Ant Farm

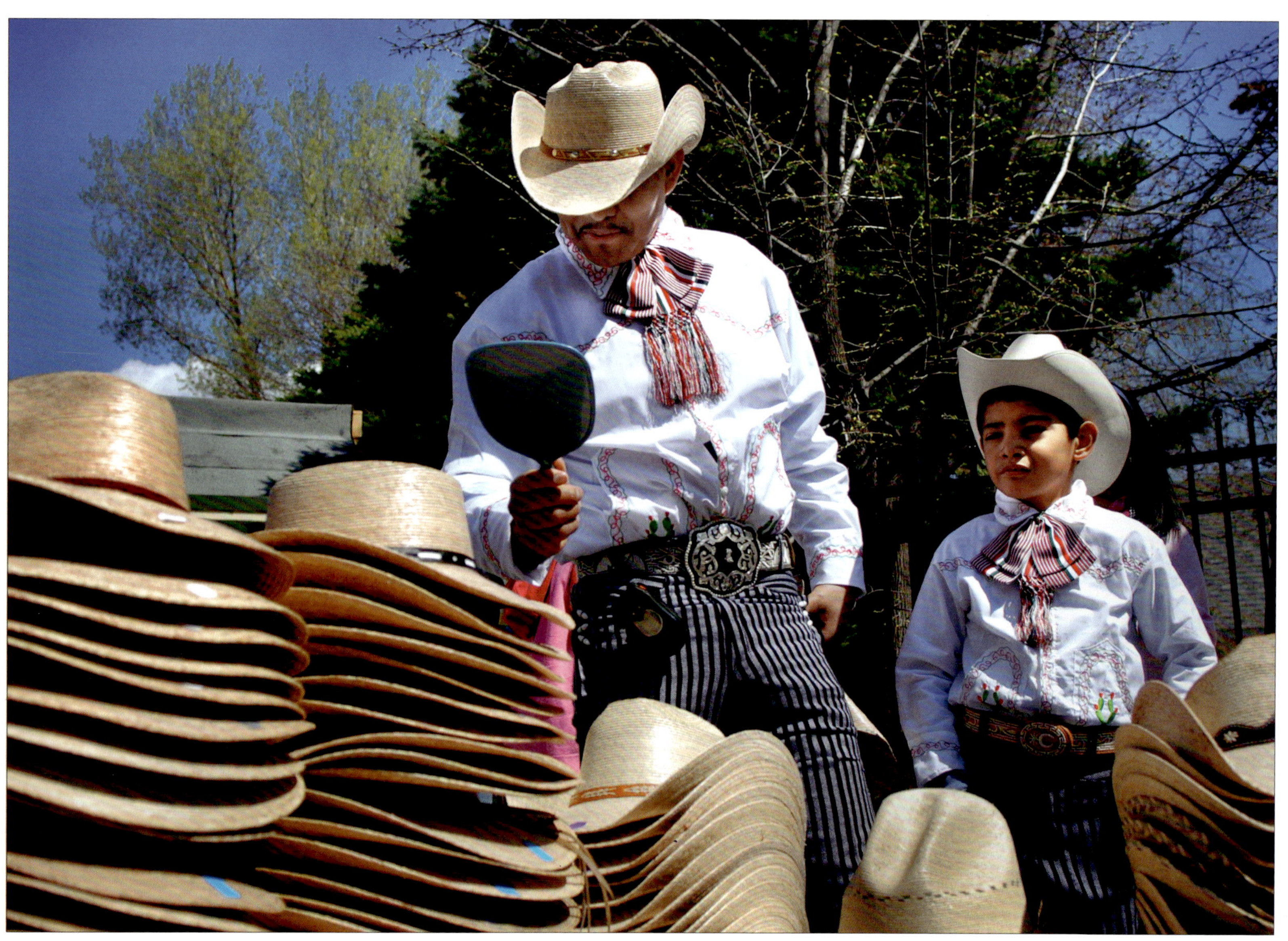

Ant Farm

Glimpses of Daily Life in Minnesota

BEN GARVIN

To Ruben!
A friend, colleague, New Yorker, story teller.
[illegible]

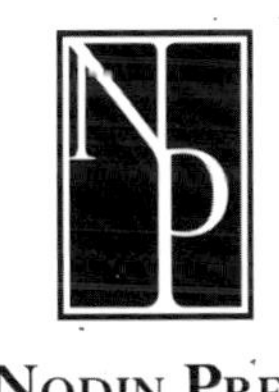

NODIN PRESS

ISBN: 978-1-932472-84-4
Library of Congress Control Number: 2009909413

Nodin Press, LLC
530 North Third Street
Suite 120
Minneapolis, MN
55401

to my wife Jessica, my best editor and best friend

Foreword

Photography has always been the art of the moment, a way of extracting something singular, and perhaps even beautiful, from the surging flux of life. Newspaper photographers—an endangered species these days—have traditionally been among the masters of this art. The best of them are visual poets of everyday life. Ben Garvin belongs to this great journalistic tradition.

Over a period of years, while working for the St. Paul *Pioneer Press* (where I was once a reporter), Garvin created a distinct body of work in a series he calls Ant Farm. Garvin's world isn't anything like the wild, violent, luridly lit realm of car crashes, murders and other assorted mayhem that once dominated newspaper photography. Nor is Ant Farm a place where you'll find images of great public spectacles—another of photojournalism's standard fares. Instead, Ant Farm is a testament to the intimate and ordinary rituals of everyday life. It's also a collection of stories in miniature, told by the subjects themselves, and their words are often as poignant as Garvin's photographs.

There is, for instance, a 30-year-old metal polisher, sitting at his machinery and staring through protective goggles at the camera. Weary of his job's repetition, he says: "Sometimes I feel like a robot, like a drone … I do the same thing day after day. I worry that my brain might turn to mush." There's a teenage girl, arms outstretched, intently practicing with two hula hoops at her family's circus studio.

"When something's not going right," she says, "when I just can't get a trick and try a hundred times, I get really mad. I don't know why." Or there's the forty-four-year-old science fiction aficionado, photographed backstage at a costume contest for which he's dressed as a character from the movie *Tron*. He speaks of the pleasure he derives from his fantasy life but also of the pain caused by online ridicule. "A couple of online stories have drawn about a thousand comments and only thirty of them have been positive. Most of the rest were along the lines of, 'Fat guys in spandex don't look good.'"

Other characters who appear in Ant Farm are equally memorable: A motorcycle enthusiast who lost both legs to a rare disease but refuses to quit riding; a seventy-seven-year-old year man who thinks his years of exposure to asbestos may finally be killing him and hopes for a quick death; a group of men square dancing at a gay rodeo; a zookeeper touching the hand of an orangutan she cares for.

In his classic book *The Face of Minnesota*, master photographer and teacher John Szarkowski distilled the essence of his art in a few simple words. The key, he wrote, is to "learn to photograph purposefully—to be less like a sponge and more like a snare." So it is with the fascinating images in this book. Garvin has done the patient, difficult work of snaring moments from the relentless rush of time, and now they are ours to see and marvel over.

– Larry Millett

Ant Farm

Nine-year-old Ryan Codner has an imaginary light-saber battle in his room in Eagan.

"Usually I pretend that I have huge things instead of normal plastic swords. It's really more funner. Say you want to have this really sweet gun that's never been invented and never will be? You can just pretend.

Once I did this mega-huge battle in my room, and it was all my white guys against half of my greens. I don't remember who won. I think they made a treaty with each other 'cause there was only three men left. And once I imagined that there was this really humongous ship that I had to blow up by myself. I put a few thermal detonators in the ship and got into a mini-ship with all my army men and flew away before it blew up.

Pretending, you can do anything."

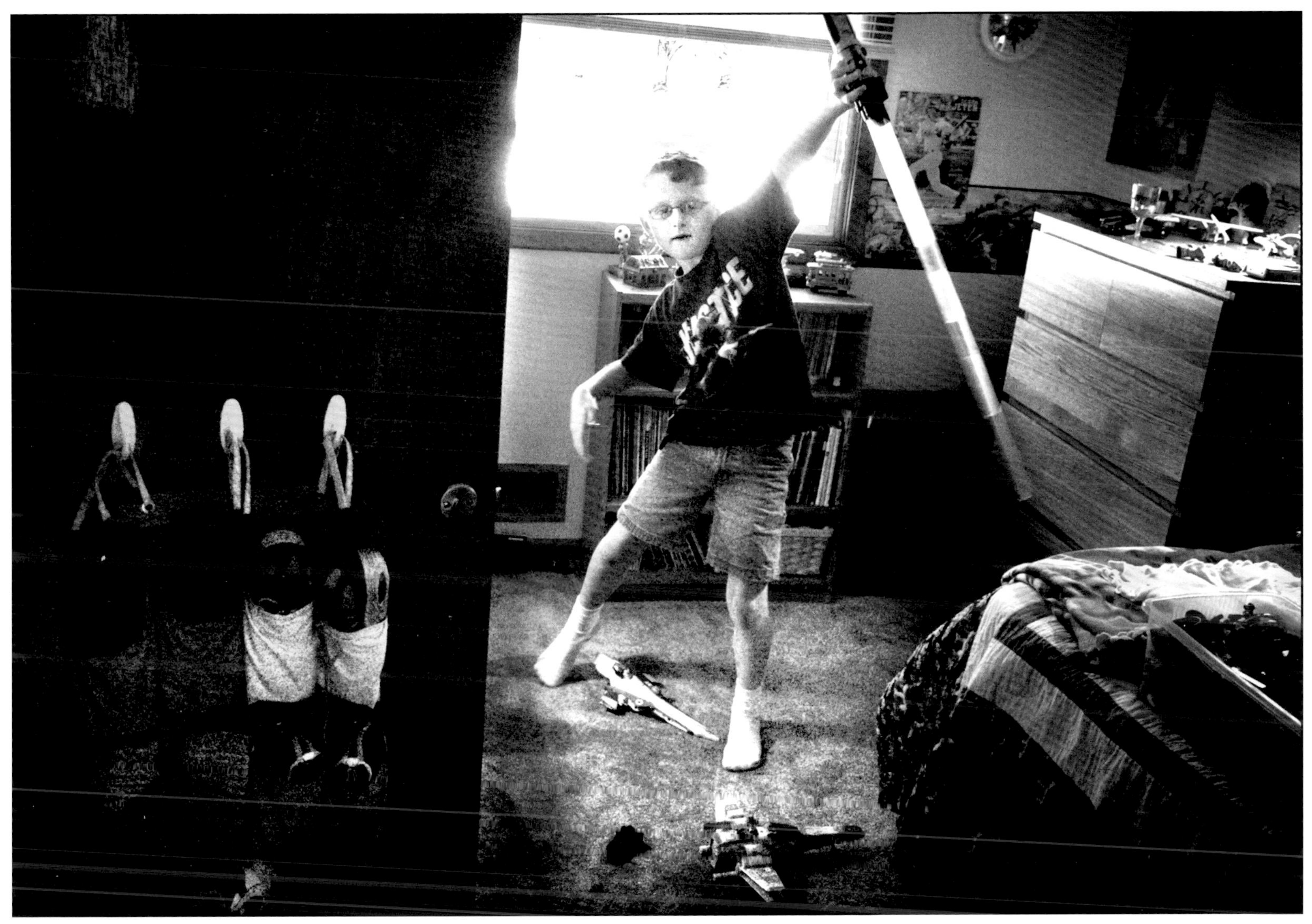

Gerry Christie, who admits to being about 70, knits a portrait of herself and a friend at her apartment in Minneapolis. She's blind.

"I never did a face before. I don't know what a face looks like. I just don't go around feeling people's faces. I know it has ears 'cause I felt mine. And I know about the eyes, even though mine don't work. I know I got a nose. I couldn't get the eyelashes right. And I never seen anybody smile. I just guessed what I think it looks like.

I've never seen me, so I don't know what I look like. I know how I feel. I love people. I like to knit. I like to sing. I don't care what my face looks like. I know people see it. There must be something there people like."

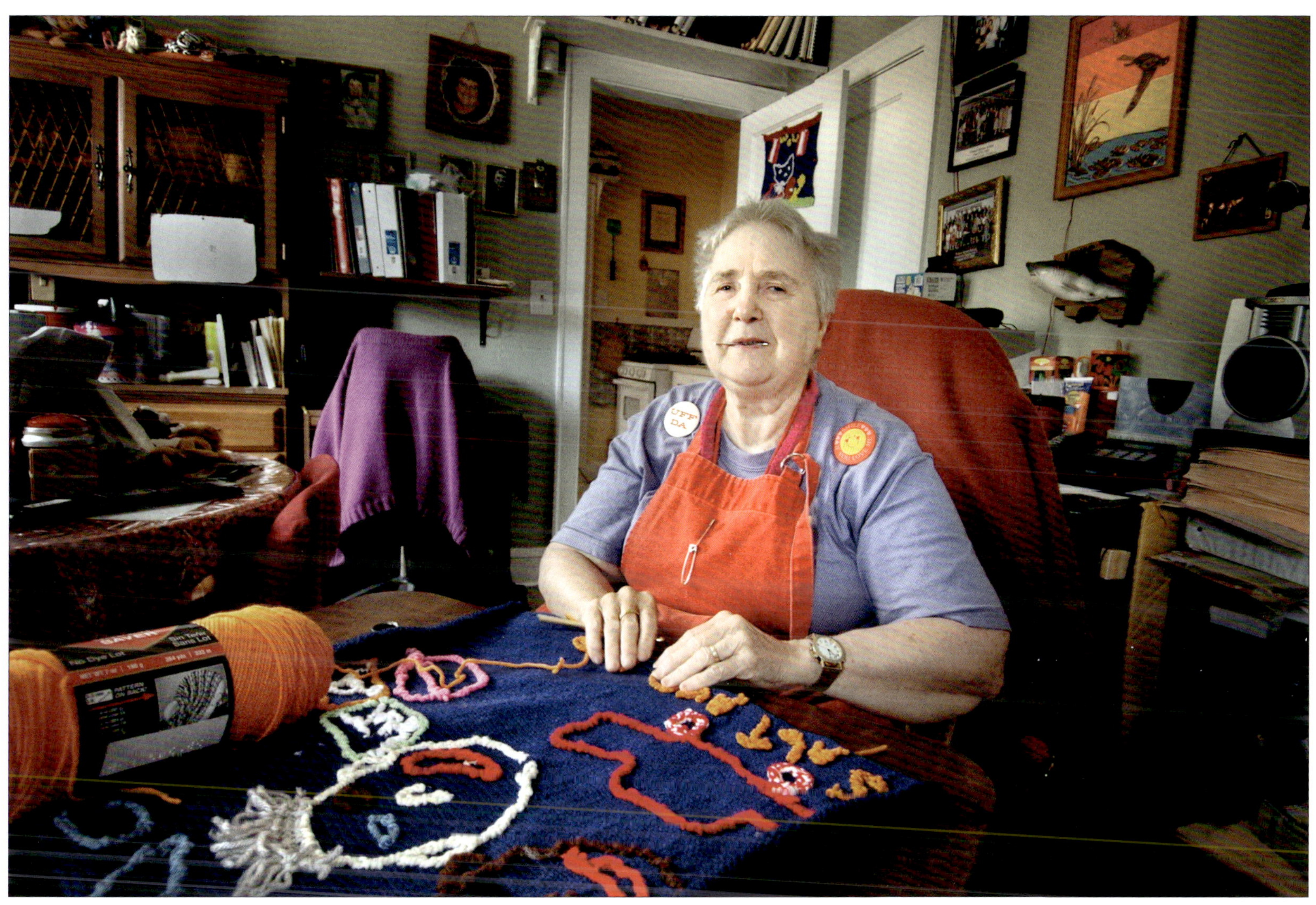
UFF
DA

Primate zookeeper Megan Elder, 29, touches the outstretched hand of Jambu, the dominant, 20-year-old, 280-pound Sumatran orangutan at the Como Zoo in St. Paul. Elder is the lead trainer of the orangutans and hopes to travel to the island of Borneo to study them in the wild.

"Jambu is my special guy. He trusts me and lets me do a lot of things that he won't let others do. He'll show me his hand, his belly; I'll actually be able to touch the surface of his teeth. He's got these huge, massive hands that could pull off my finger in a minute, but he's very gentle.

Sometimes I lose sight of our differences because orangutans are so much like us—their personalities, their intelligence, their curiosity. If they were able to get ahold of my keys they would unlock every door in the facility. They know what locks are. They check them every day. If you give a female a brush and some warm soapy water, she'll go to town cleaning the exhibits.

It's a privilege to be able to work so closely with these guys. I want to see them in the wild before they go extinct, to help in any way I can with research and to help them survive longer. When I was a little girl, I wanted to work with dolphins like so many others. But while I was in college, I gained an appreciation for all the other animal groups out there. I got more into conservation. Every living being on this planet somehow affects the next. We're all connected in this whole web of life. Is that deep or what?"

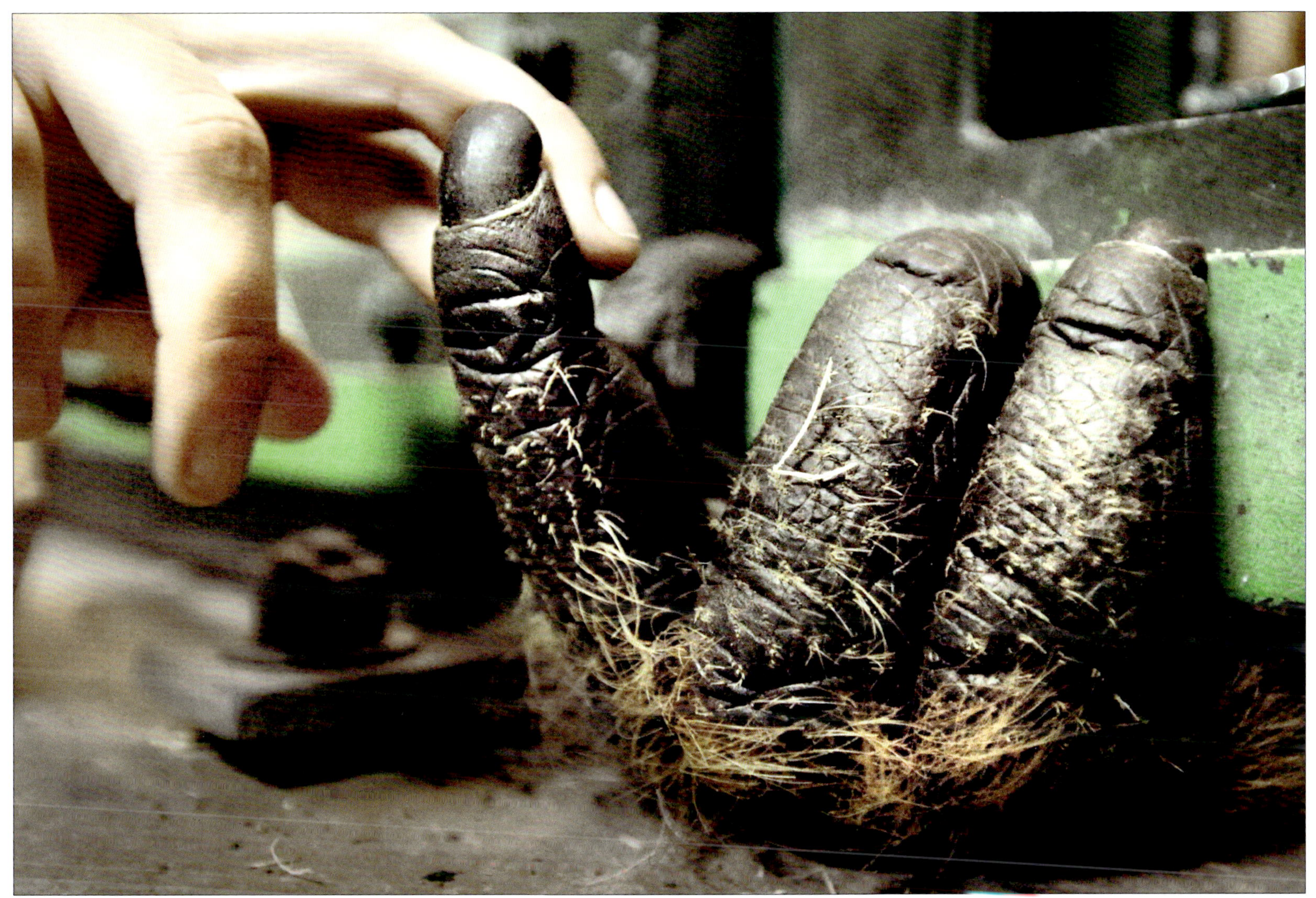

Lois Graff, center, wins another hand of royal rummy during a biweekly gathering of widows in Oakdale.

"When my husband died, I wondered if I should stay in the house or not. That's a question most women have. It seems like at least two years before a woman is ready to go out and do things socially after her husband dies. It didn't take me that long 'cause I had a friend who wanted to learn square dancing.

And then I thought, well, I have all this outside work to do, so I learned how to mow the lawn and take care of his gardens. He had seven gardens. One by one, those have been turned into rock or grass. I only have one garden left, and it's mostly taken over by raspberries.

One thing I like about not being married is that I can make my decisions without consulting somebody. There's freedom, freedom to do things and make my own way. If I want to stay up all night or read until four in the morning, I can. I like this independent life."

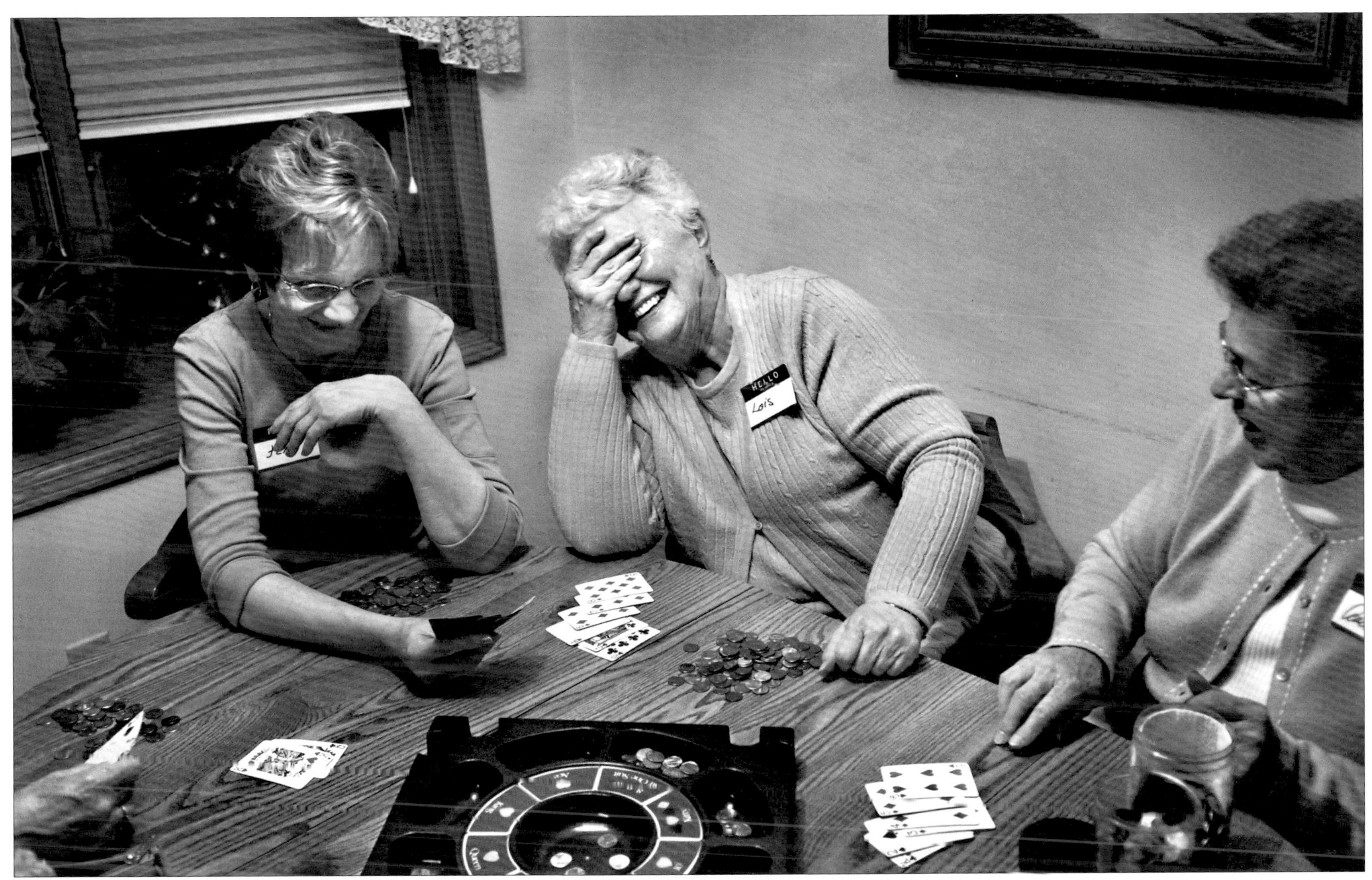
HELLO
Lois

During their weekly meeting for worship at the Friends School of Minnesota in St. Paul—an independent Quaker school—first-graders do their best to remain still. At right is head Mark Niedermier. From left in front row: Aaron Corpstein, Marina Vernick, Tessa Newman-Heggie and Mei Li.

"During worship, sometimes I count how many people are in half the class. And all the teachers, too. And sometimes I see how many new people are there.

And sometimes I see how many candles are there. This time there were, like, five or six candles. And sometimes I just daydream.

I daydream about when it's going to be over and when is the end of school and what day is it. Sometimes I daydream about recess and what I'm going to play. I like to hide on the playground and spy on people and write about them in my notebook. I have a hiding spot most people know. Well, all people know. I hide right there.

And sometimes I daydream about sleeping."

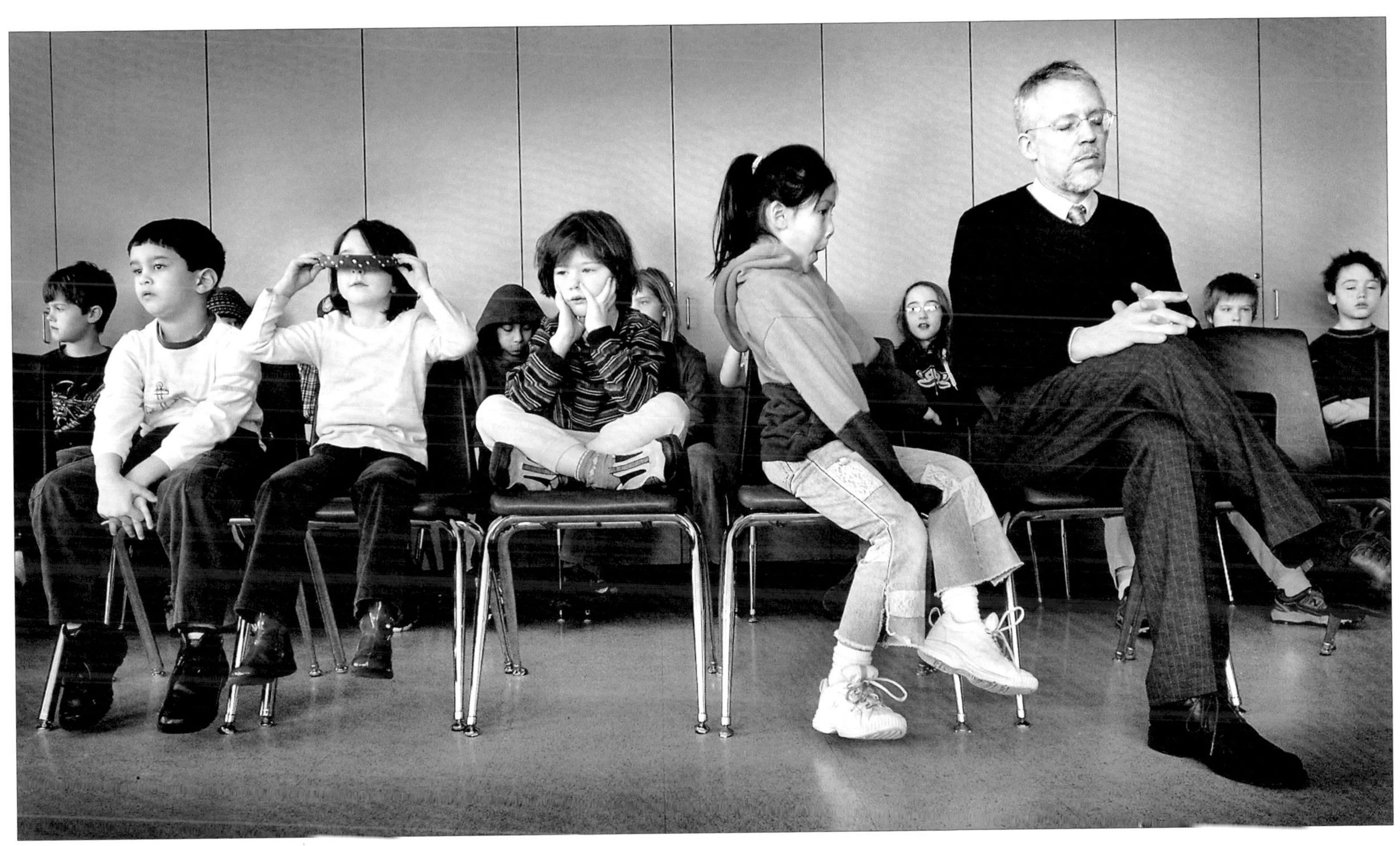

Nemo Gannon, 22, adjusts his hair at the Saloon bar in Minneapolis during a Goth prom.

"Because it was a Goth prom, I decided to go more androgynous and wear a long, floor-length skirt, black-vinyl cincher and some fishnets.

I like to mix my outfits. One of my favorites is, like, Gothic vinyl pants with new rock boots and a ceremonial Chinese gown that I acquired from someone who went to China. Seeing the long dress with a deep crimson red dragon on it, with really tall platforms and the vinyl pants—it's really beautiful.

The way we dress, we're usually poster boys for fear. But there's nothing to be afraid of; this has nothing to do with being evil or being sadistic. It's a creative outlet, a statement of who we are."

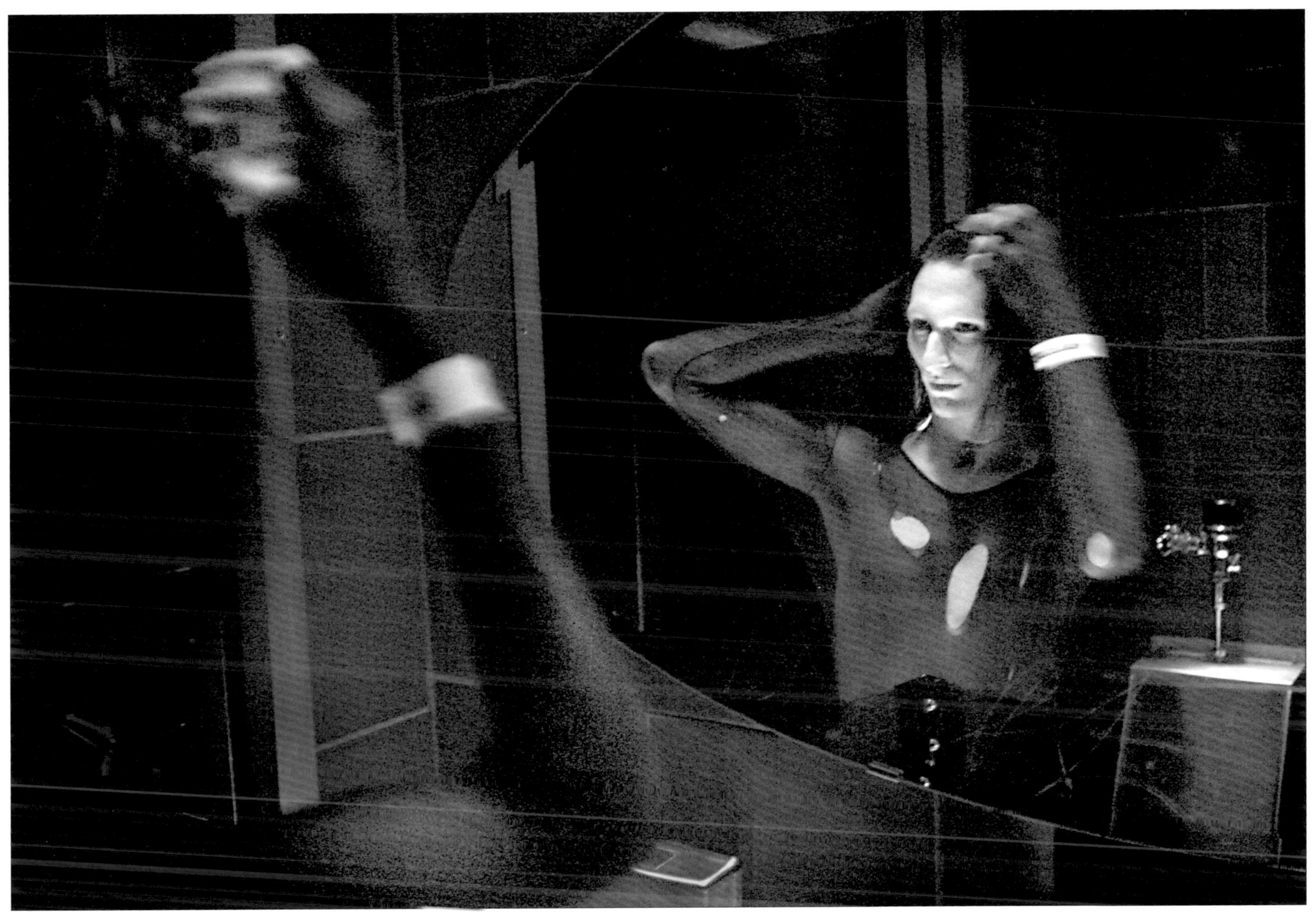

Thomas Nelson Jr., a maintenance man for Xcel Energy, works with his eight-year-old son, Thomas Nelson III, to fix a broken ball joint on a friend's car in Minneapolis.

"Ever since he was one or two years old, he went along with me to fix things. 'Dad, take me,' he says. 'I just want to be around you.' And either I spend time with my kids or somebody else will, you know? So he watches and picks up his own perspective on how to do things.

I'm surprised by some of the things he figures out. Sometimes his sisters are like, 'Dad, Thomas tore up our toys!' But you have to break some eggs before you make an omelet."

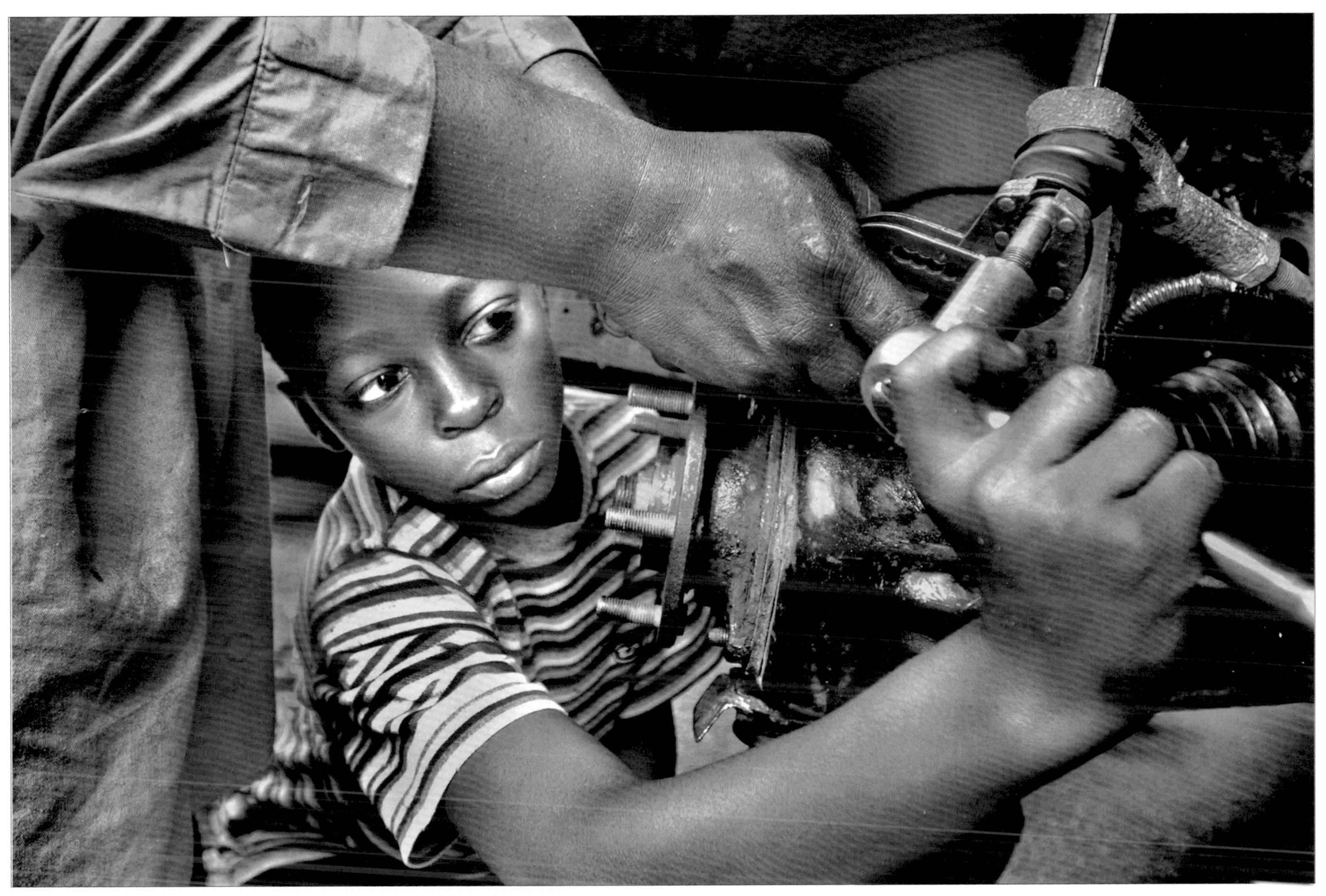

Steve Nord, 53, photographs high school baseball players before the start of a tournament in Chaska. Nord, who suffered a stroke 15 years ago after a car accident, shoots amateur sports and makes the images available for $1.50 on his Web site: rollingphoto.com.

"My dream lens is a 300mm 2.8; I'm saving up. My wife said I got to sell a lot more pictures and charge more. Everybody says 'You gotta raise it! You gotta raise it!' But you know, I would rather sell a ton of pictures at a low price than a few at a high price. I just want everybody to have one.

The really good athletes don't have to worry about getting their picture taken, but players that are less in the limelight, being in a tournament's a big time for them, too. And it's a big time for their parents. So I try to get a few good ones of everybody.

Once a mom said to me, 'My son's team won that tournament, and you got very few pictures of him. He was the catcher.' And then I just felt terrible! I felt like I had let her down. So later, I heard that they were playing again in St. Cloud, and I went up and just hammered the heck out of her son: in the dugout, putting his pads on, batting, throwing a guy out, everything. She bought a whole ton of them."

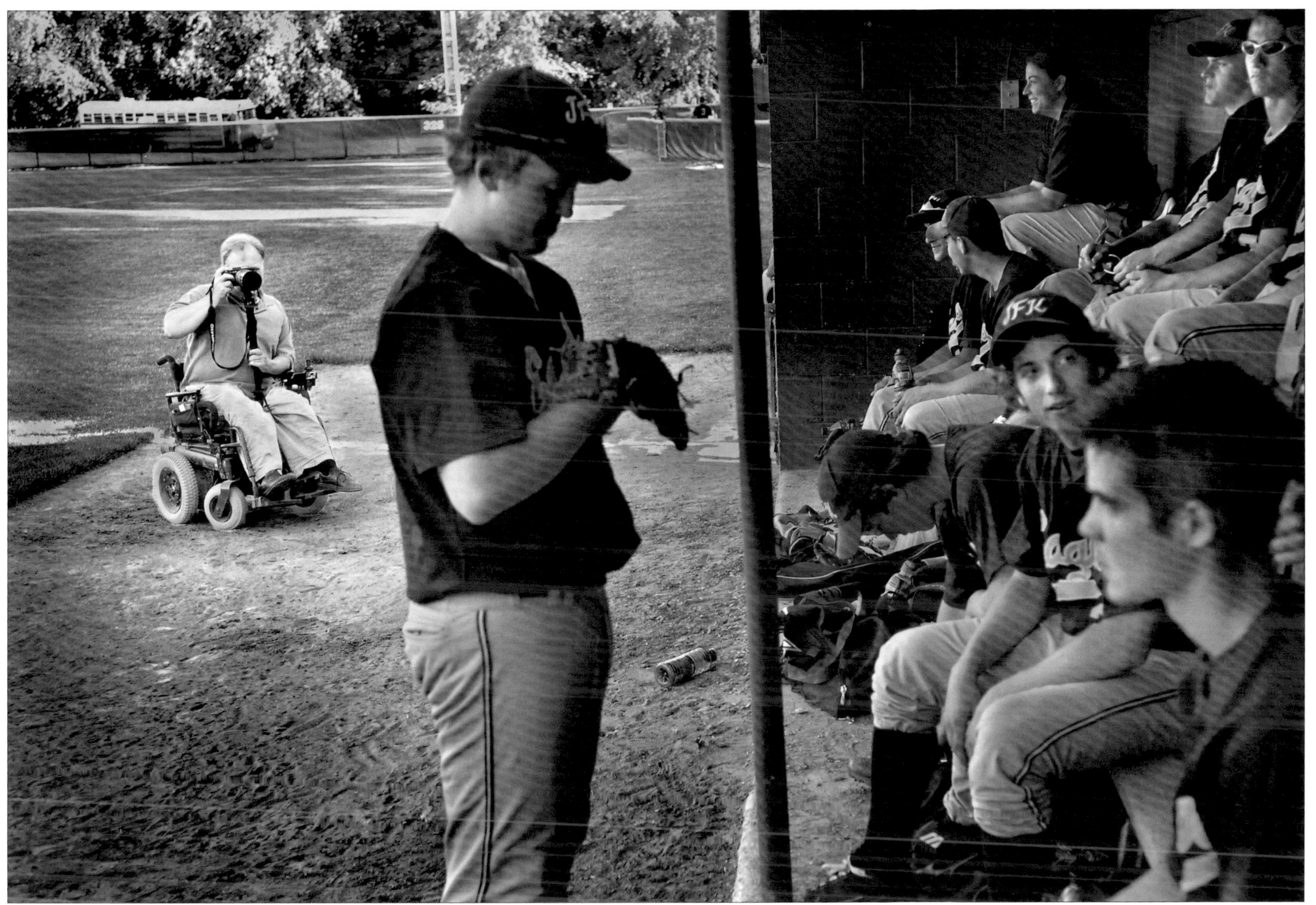
JFK

Eighty-two-year-old Robbe Vanouse gets ready to roll his 13-pound ball at a bowling ally in St. Paul. At age 75, he bowled a perfect game—12 strikes in a row.

"It was winter. I can't remember, I think it was December … 22nd. At Maplewood Bowling Alley there, over at Frost and English, if you know where that is. I don't know if it was deserved or not, but I did bowl quite a few years to get that. Been bowling since right after I got out of the war in '46.

I don't wear my 300-ring all the time, but when I bowl, I do. Or when we go out to eat or something. The average guy, what does he do in his lifetime? Maybe he makes a hole in one? Maybe he gets a 300 game. What else can you do? That's what I got as my claim to fame."

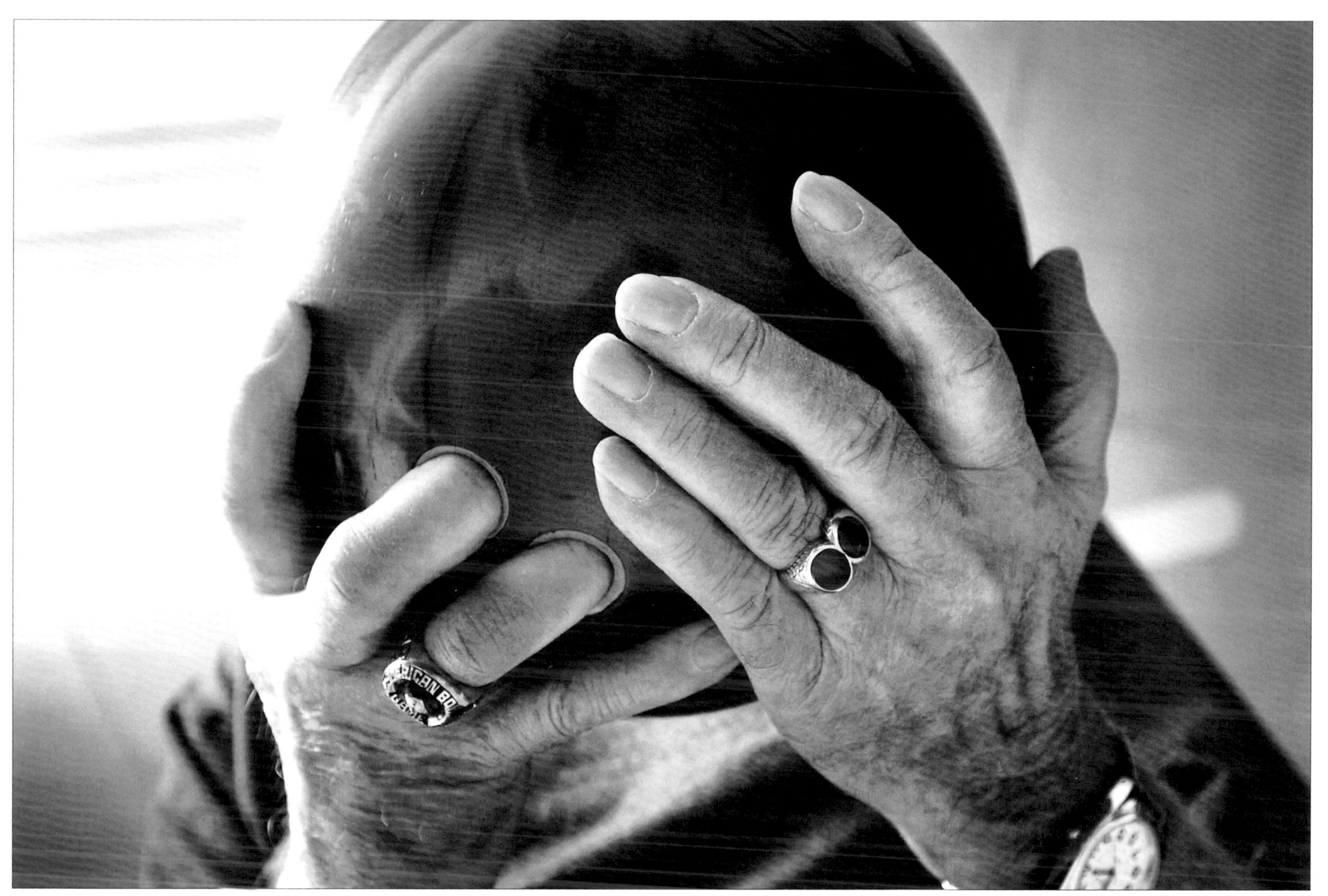

Steve Doyle, 19, receives a foot choke during pro wrestling practice in a friend's back yard in Maplewood. He's a member of Northern Impact Wrestling, a group of young wrestlers who put on shows in parking lots around St. Paul.

"My classmates were really into basketball, but I have the coordination of a skunk on ice when it comes to that game. I always felt like everyone else knew what was going on, and I wasn't quite getting it, you know?

Being a part of wrestling was finally something I could do that no one else could. It was kind of awkward at first—I'm usually a shy guy—but once I got in there it was fun, sharing some jokes, ribbing each other. I felt like I belonged somewhere.

Actually, four of my groomsmen are going to be these guys—three wrestlers and a ref."

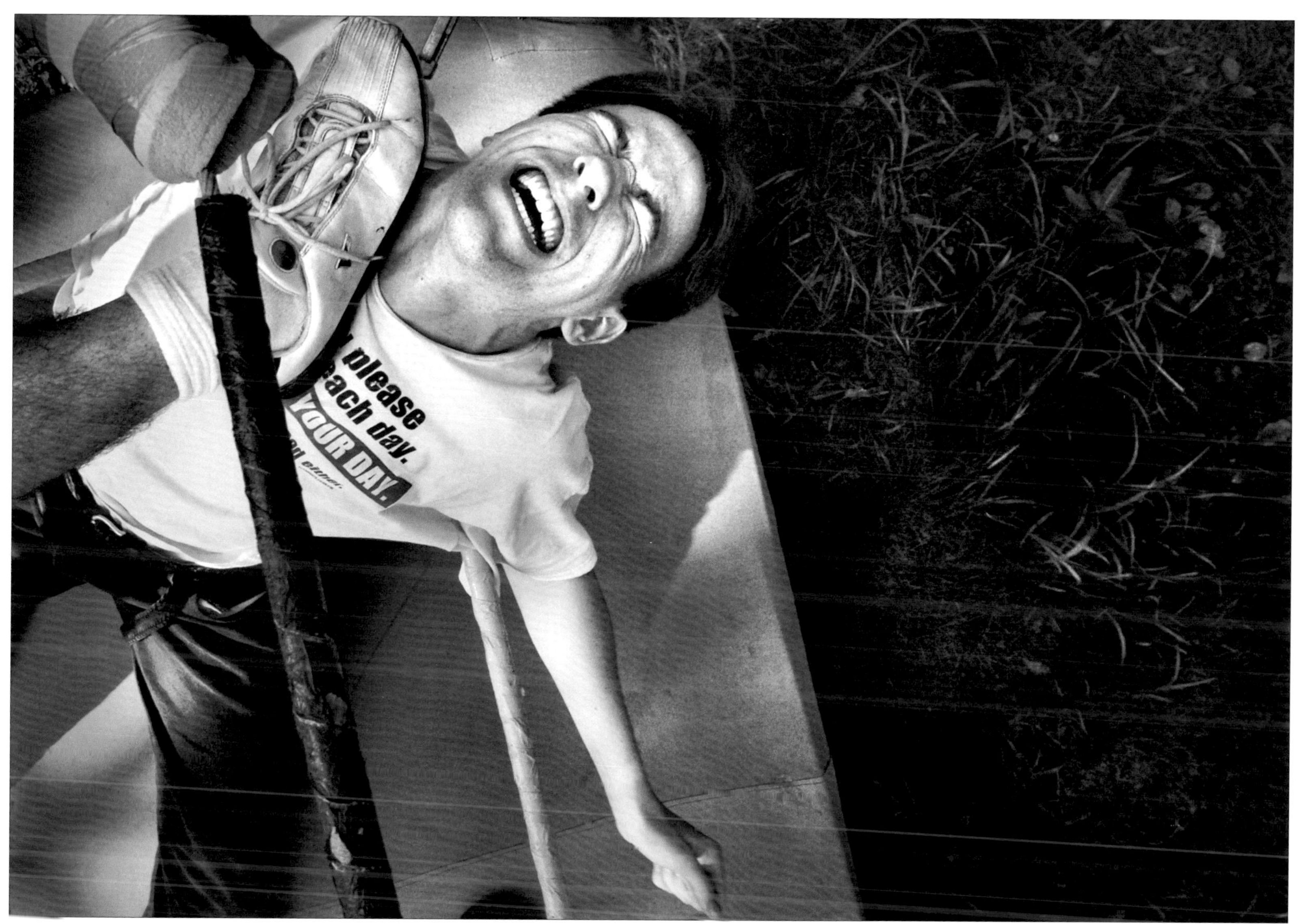
please
each day.
YOUR DAY.

St. Paul: Pastor **Luches Hamilton**, 55, tends to his chicken and ribs at Pastor Hamilton's Bar-B-Que in St. Paul. Profits go to St. John's Church, where he's pastor.

"Good barbecue, it takes time. You can't rush it. I'm from Arkansas, and we made good barbecue by just digging a hole in the ground. We didn't know what a grill was.

We put iron rods across the hole and put the pig on it. We cover him up with corn shucks and put a blanket over it and throw the dirt back on there and leave a hole just big enough to put the hickory wood down there.

We would leave it in the ground for three days. Three days!

Then we'd pull the blanket back off, take the shucks off and get a pail with sauce. Get a white sheet, rip it up, tie it on a stick and mop that pig. The sauce would drip down into the fire. When it would run off and hit the coals, it would send up that nice aroma. That's what gives the flavor.

When we brought the pig to the table, the meat just fell off the bone. *That* was good barbecue."

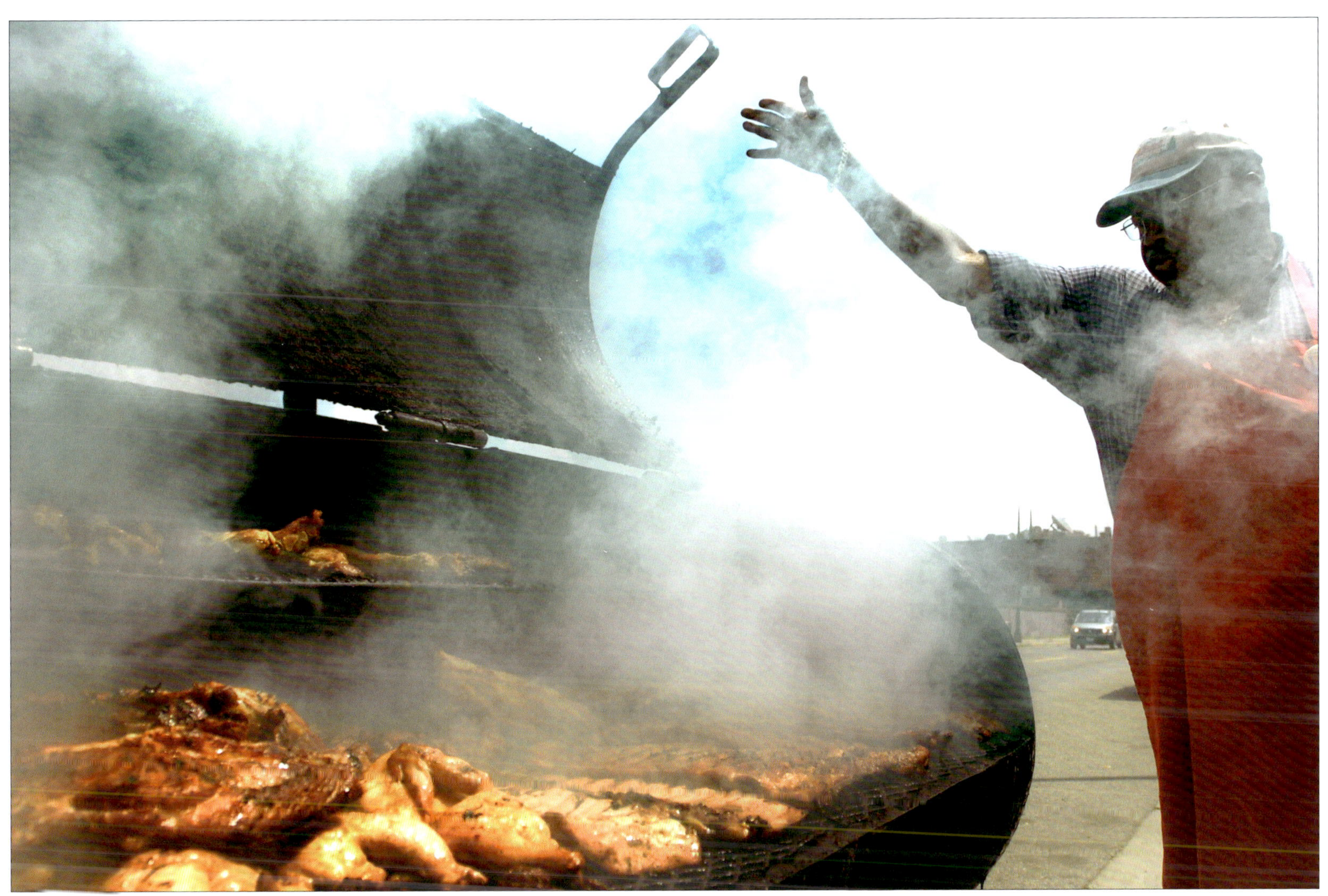

In his living room in St. Paul, Warren "Golden" Walker Jr., 40, holds up *Glitterbest*, one of his favorite glam rock compilations of all time. He found the album on a recent trip to San Francisco, where he went to find classic recordings of the genre.

"When I found *Shine on Silver Light* by Hello, I was amazed. I was looking for it for years and finally found it for $25 plus shipping. I usually take a nap when I come home from work, but when I saw it in the mail, I thought, 'Not today.'

I'm not just in it for its rarity, but the sound. Glam's all about the beat, that percussion crunchin' beat. It's got that youthful enthusiasm to it. Just like myself. I'm the type that goes for the gusto. All out, a hundred percent.

I don't understand why people go for normal, regular stuff. Either you're ordinary or you're extraordinary. Either you're gonna settle for regular, average-sounding stuff or you're gonna get the pinnacle of music, the top level, the loft, the 'upper crust' as the Brits would say. That's glam."

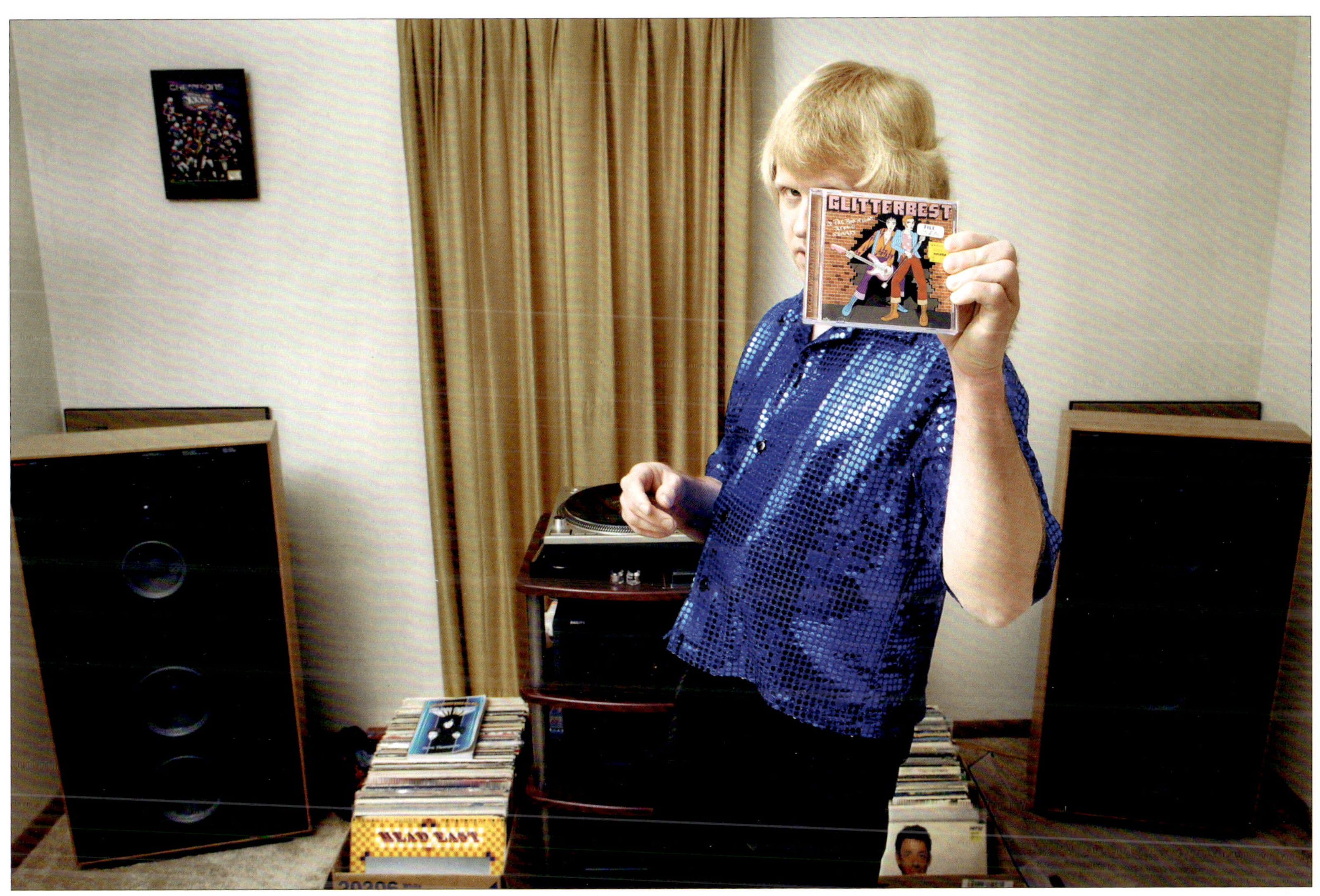
GLITTERBEST
HEAD EAST

On her first day of school eight-year-old Jessika Faehn lines up for lunch with other third-graders in Mr. VanAlstine's class at Rice Lake Elementary in Lino Lakes.

"When it was the last day of summer, which was yesterday, I was just so excited that I slept only a little bit. I woke up at like three or five in the morning. The bus was a little late, so I started getting a little upset, but then when I got to school I got so, so happy because I was so happy. I couldn't believe that I had to wait for a whole entire summer for school to start!

Every single time I move up a grade, I get a little nervous. There are lots and lots of math problems, and this year I have to learn cursive. I'm hoping more geography, because that's what I'm really eager about. Like traveling north and west, west and east, and south. Northeast and southeast, and northwest and southwest.

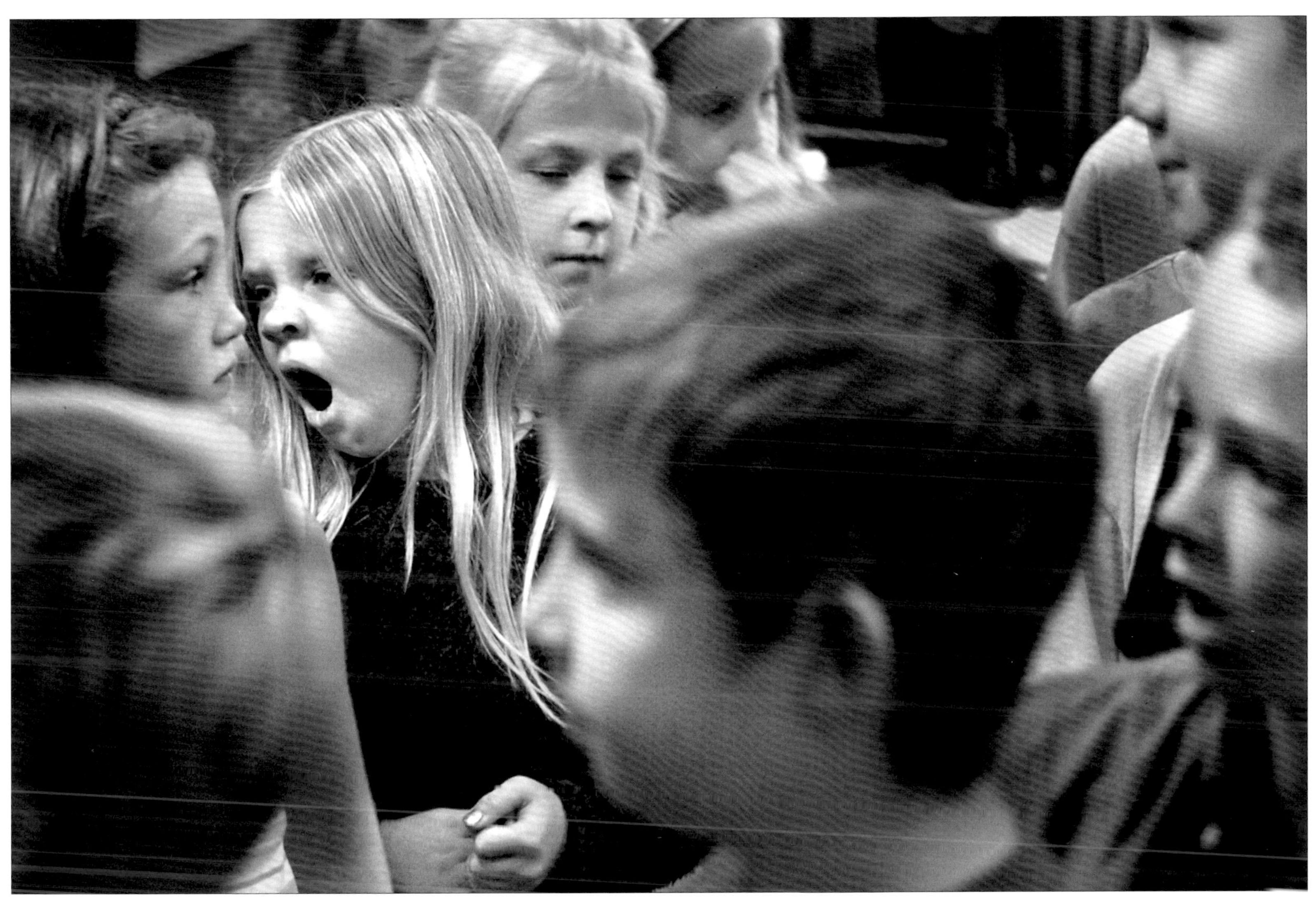

Fourteen-year-old Ben Hebert laughs during a Jeopardy-style science review game led by his special education teacher, Teresa Wieler, at Maplewood Middle School. "With Ben, he seems to actually be internally happy," said Wieler. "It's not that he doesn't feel anger or feel hurt; he just chooses to be happy, and I just find that amazing."

"I'm tall. I just like to be tall. Other people are short and I'm tall. I'm the tallest in my family. I'm taller than my dad and my big brother and my mom.

I like all my classes, and I like all the teachers. Even the principal. I just like to be friendly. It's nice to be nice and that's it.

If I could change one thing in my life, I'd make kids at school stop calling me names. 'Retard.' I don't like it; I'm not a retard. They think I am, but I'm not. I don't get mad and I don't say nothing. I feel sad inside and I just want to say, 'Stop it,' but I just be quiet.

I wish President Bush would get the newspaper with me in it. That would be cool. And I would go and visit him someday.

'President Bush, do you have the paper of me?'
'Yeah, what's your name, kid?' And I might say, 'My name is Ben.' "

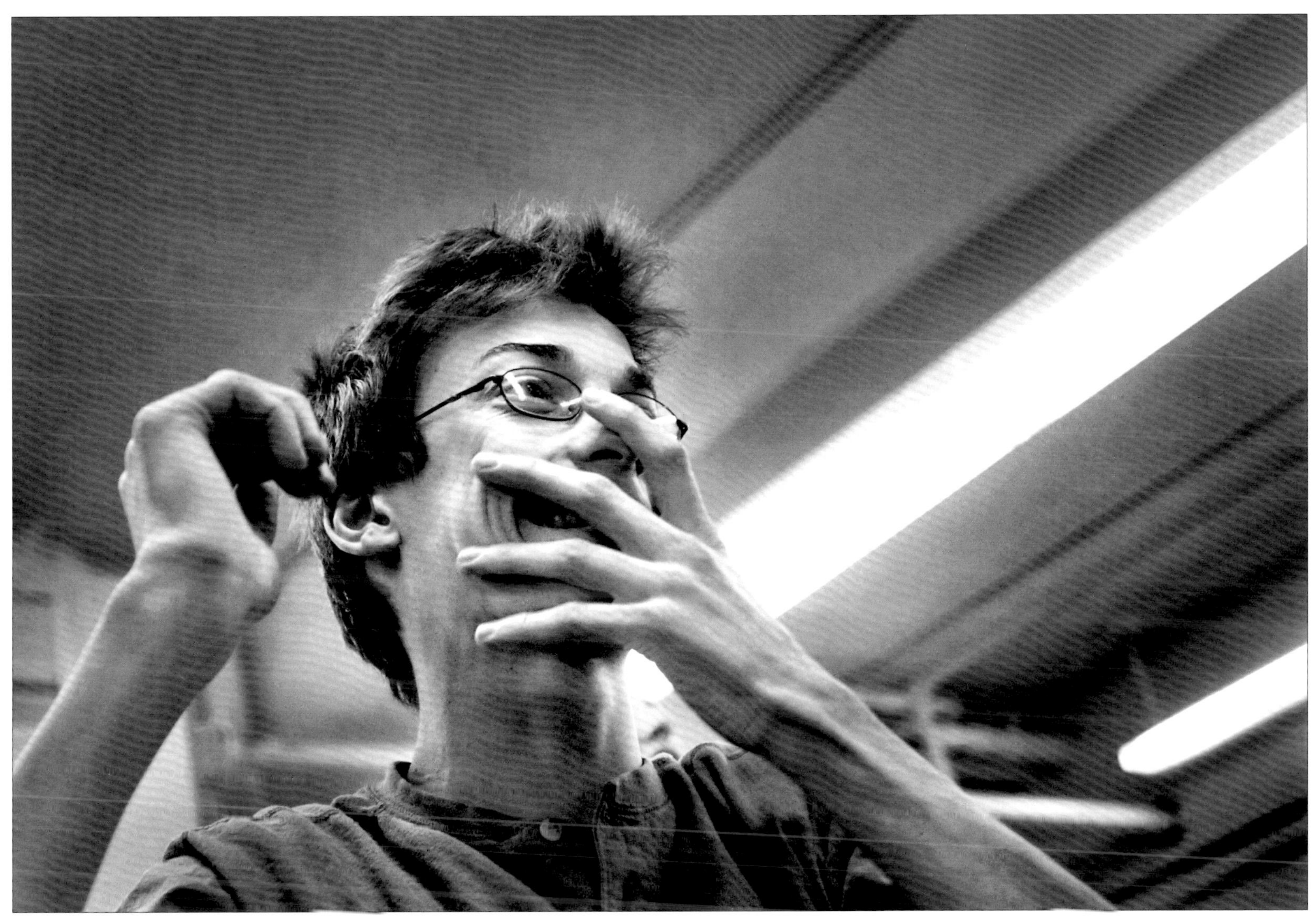

Aaron Holt, 16, practices clogging between filling the horses' water bucket and feeding the pigs on his farm in Center City.

"It is easy to be afraid of what people think when you're performing. I used to set up pillows and put hats and jackets on them, and it would make them look like bizarre humans, and so that helped me get over my fear. Then, I moved on to my family sitting in front of me while I performed. And then, I moved on to higher levels of crowdage, like the classroom, then the auditorium. And just about two years ago, I had to sing at the State Fair, and that was in front of a huge crowd of people. That took guts. I sang "Can You Feel the Love Tonight" by Elton John. I kept good eye contact and kept smiling and just went right through it. I got a red ribbon for that.

People are talking nowadays that I could be a role model for people. I'm like, whoa, I've never heard that before. I'm not sure what it's like, but I think I want to give it a try."

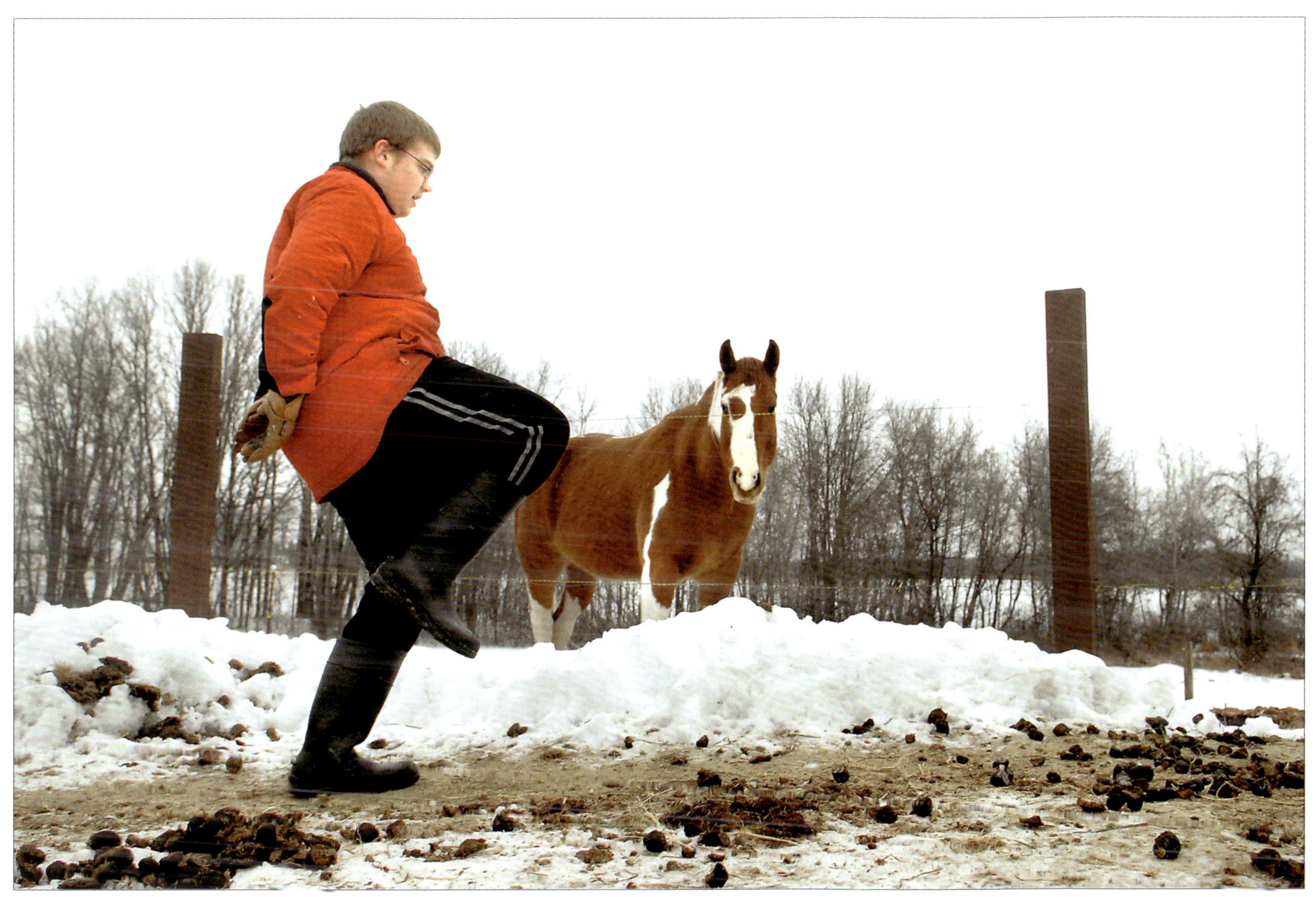

The man who goes by Limo pours barbecue sauce over a bratwurst he cooked in the hot asphalt truck he drives. After double-wrapping his food in aluminum foil, he buries it in the asphalt and later digs it out, fully cooked.

"When they told me that the temperature was 340° on the blacktop, I thought, 'Mom sets the oven for 350° and I'm pretty close.' So I started out by seeing if I could do steaks. They cook, but you have to have a big driveway so you can let the truck sit—they need two hours cooking time. Then I asked myself, 'What else could I do if I try?' I've cooked ribs, pork chops, broccoli and cheese, dinner rolls, buttermilk biscuits, sweet corn, peach pie, quiche, omelets.

How I do an omelet is a secret.

They still blame the driveway we had to redo in St. Louis Park on my pork going through the paver. I couldn't get my radio to work to tell my co-worker to get my pork out of the 57,000-pound stove before he dumped my truck. I get back and they're all holding a couple pieces of pork here and there from all over the place. The paver just spit it all over. They've never let me hear the end of it."

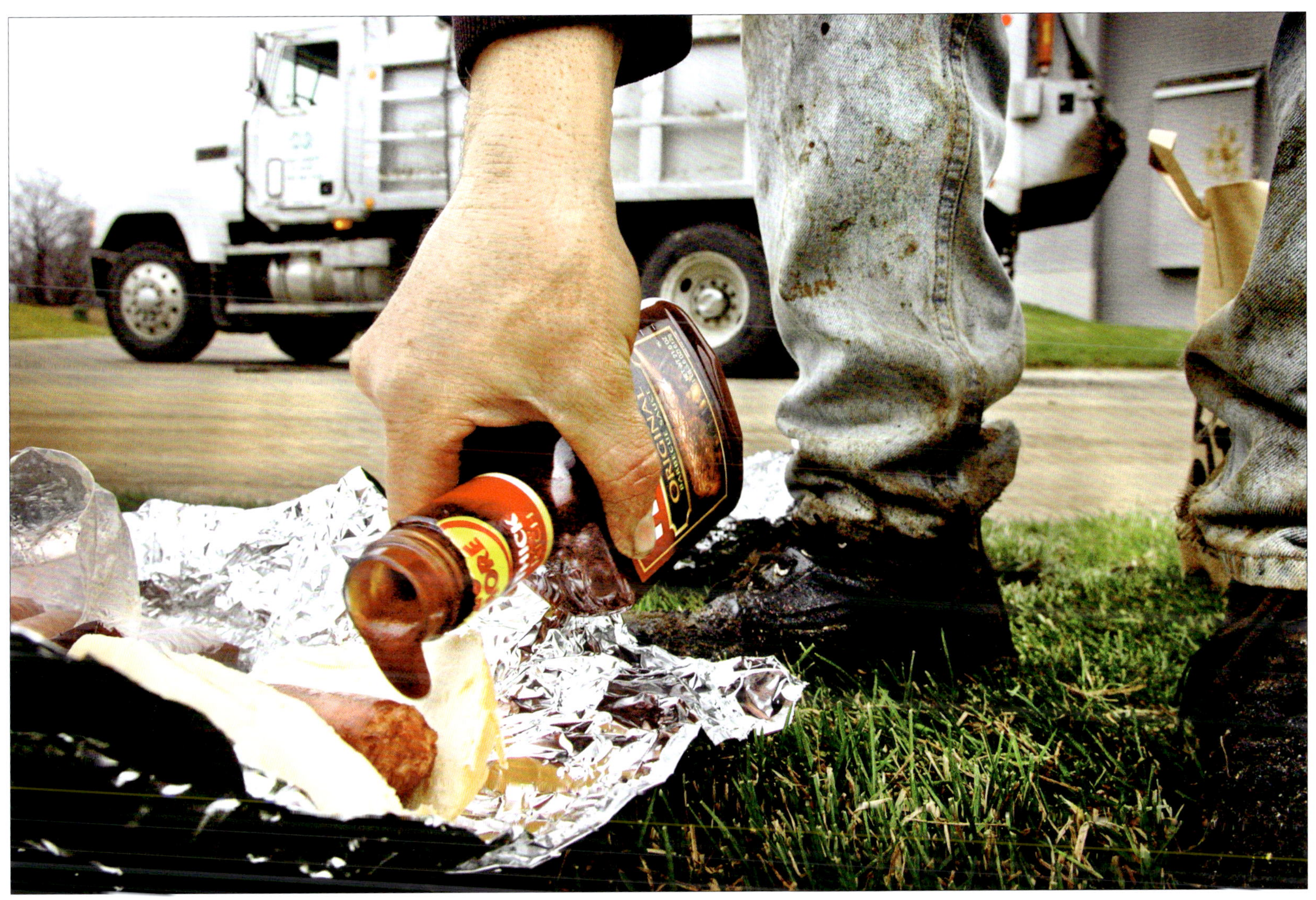
ORIGINAL

Aerial Emery, 15, practices tricks with her hula hoops in her family's circus studio in Roseville.

"When something's not going right, when I just can't get a trick and try a hundred times, I get really mad. I don't get why. I'll throw a hoop and just storm out of the studio and sit in my room, put on Beatles, chill out.

My dad will be like, 'How'd it go?' and I'll be like, 'Horrible!' He understands.

Both my parents are amazing performers. They lived in a circus train for three years, and it sounds like the most fun that could ever be had. After high school, I don't want to go to college. I want to go to circus school or be in a traveling circus. I want to do something with a circus, anything."

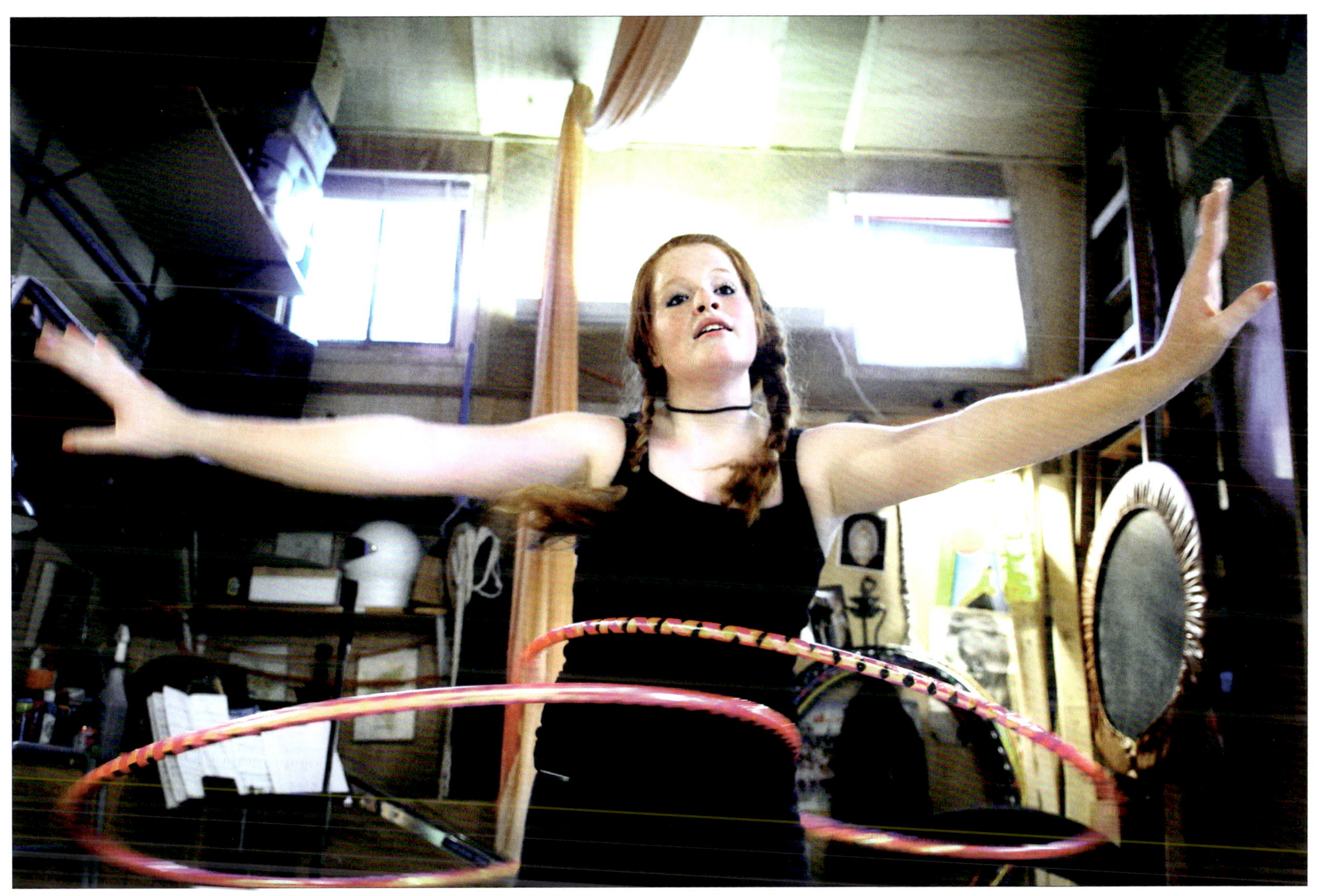

Frank Saunby, 27, waits for a bite while ice fishing on Lake Phalen in St. Paul.

"I used to just sit and listen to my dad and my grandpa tell fish stories out here on the lake. My dad would walk out and show me all the spots to catch fish. I don't have GPS and the cameras and stuff, so I gotta go by remembering what my grandpa and dad said, where they caught them.

Yesterday, I was out here catching fish all day long. Other guys were looking over, and they'd get a little closer and a little closer. When I left, I saw about five people move to where I was fishing and start drilling holes.

I don't mind. It makes me feel a little good. If people, older people, are following me around the lake and I'm only 27, it makes me feel like a good fisherman. They got all the high-tech gear, and I'm just out here with an ice auger and bucket, and I'm catching fish."

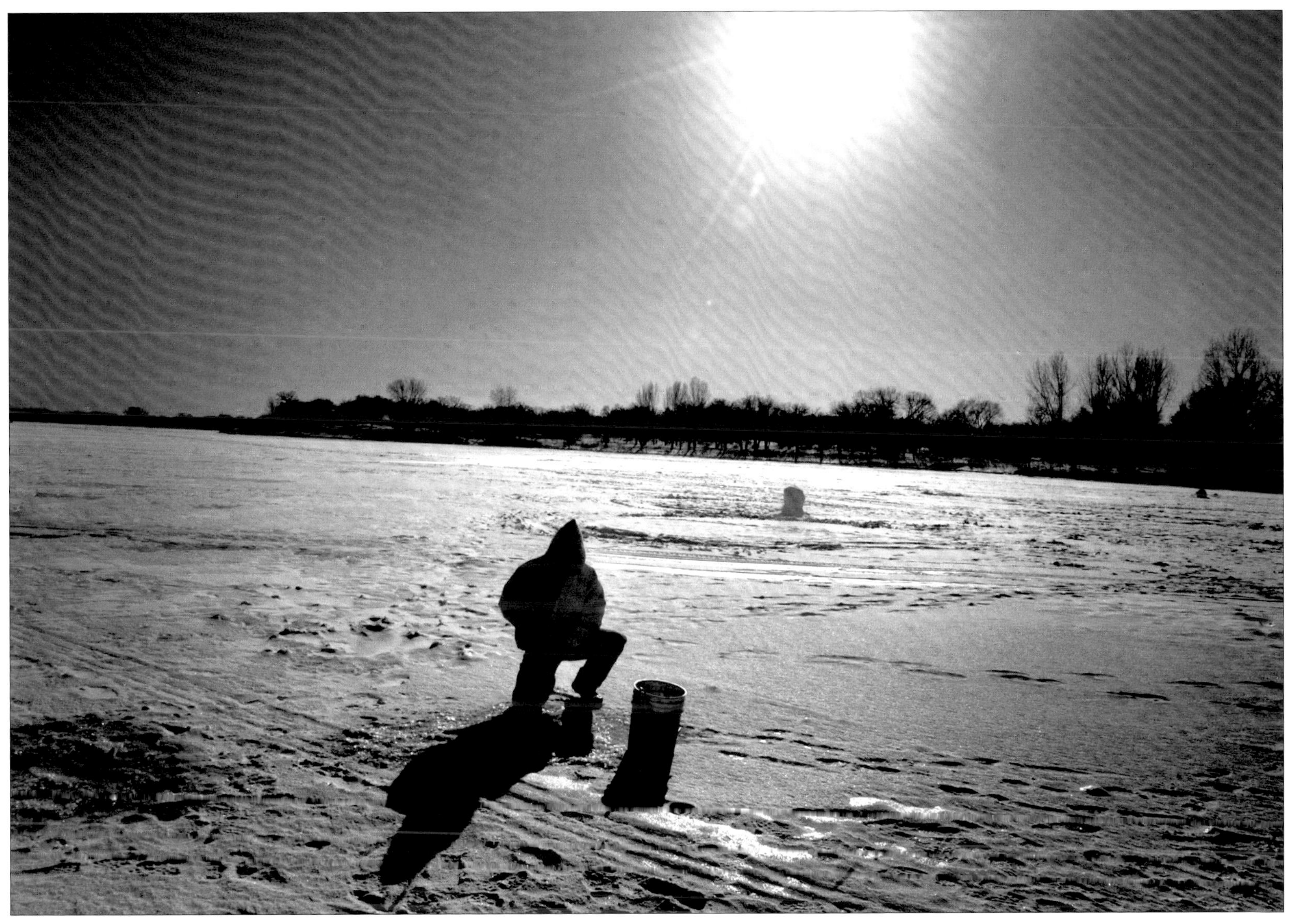

Matt Milosevich, 21, guides a group of heifers into the auction ring at Central Livestock in South St. Paul.

"Sometimes you get cows that are just mad at the world. Last week, we had a bad Brahma bull come in, and we couldn't get him down the alley. He was down at one end hittin' the fence, trying to get these guys on the other side, so I jumped out in the alley with him and started pawing the ground and yelling at him and he turned around and come runnin' at me.

So, instead of jumping out, I just run down the alley, and he was coming after me, and then I ran right into what we call the 'pocket,' right before they go into the ring, and I jumped up on the gate and flipped over.

He went in the ring, and they sold him. I don't remember how much, but, I mean, he got butchered."

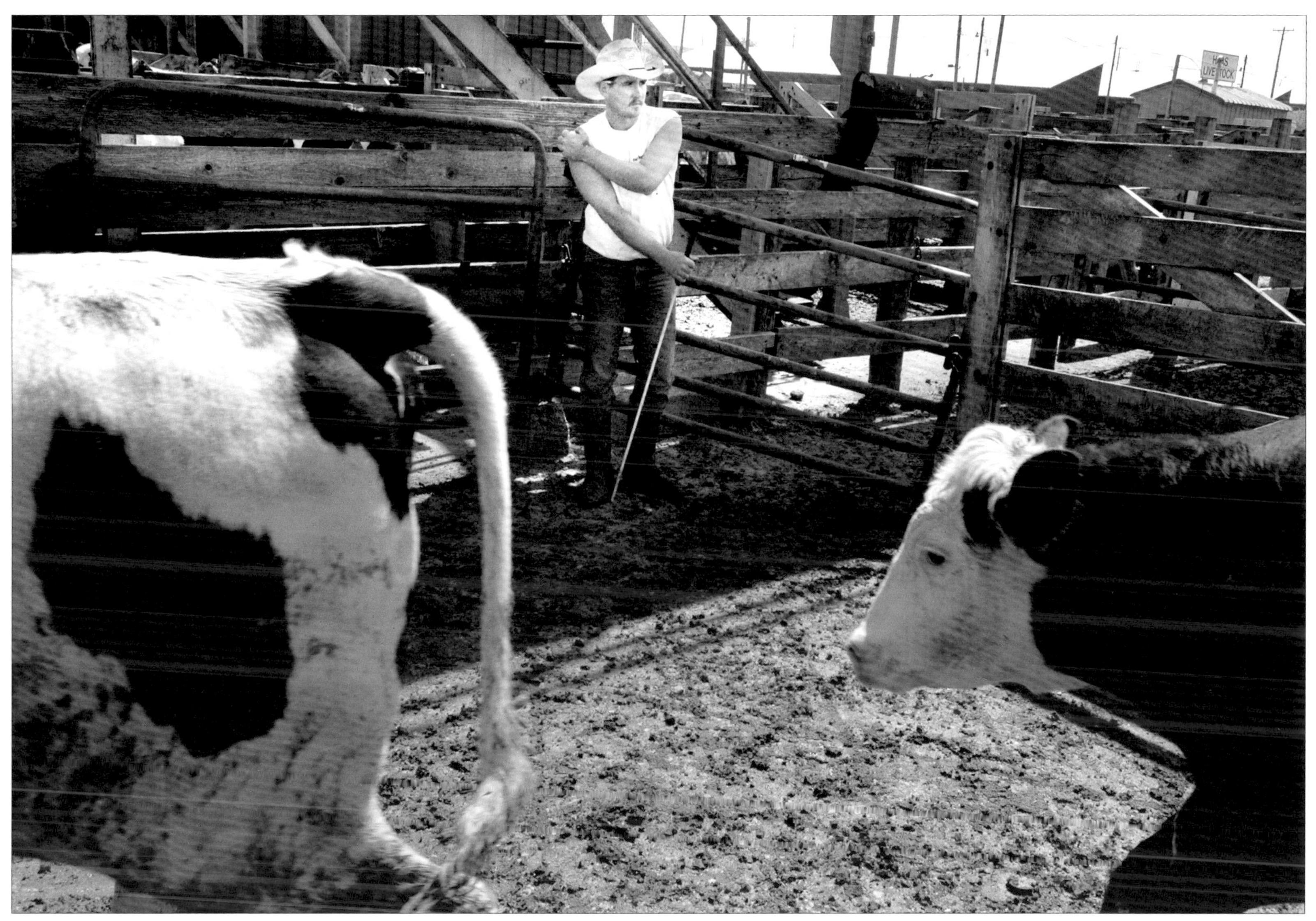

Brian Thompson, 40, has Pam cooking oil applied to his legs before competing in the Mr. Minnesota Bodybuilding Championship. He won first place in the masters category.

"Bodybuilding has nothing to do with performance. It's all aesthetics. To look this way, you go beyond feeling good. I've dieted for 16 weeks. No milk, no bread, no dairy products. It's all just fish, chicken, egg whites and complex carbs. As I got closer to the show, there was less salmon. Then oatmeal went out. I was constantly entering new levels of suffering. At the very end, I went five days in a row with zero carbs. Just chicken breasts. I had seven chicken breasts a day.

When I'm all depleted I kind of get emotional. I'm kind of a softy. I have a friend who calls me the Iron Marshmallow."

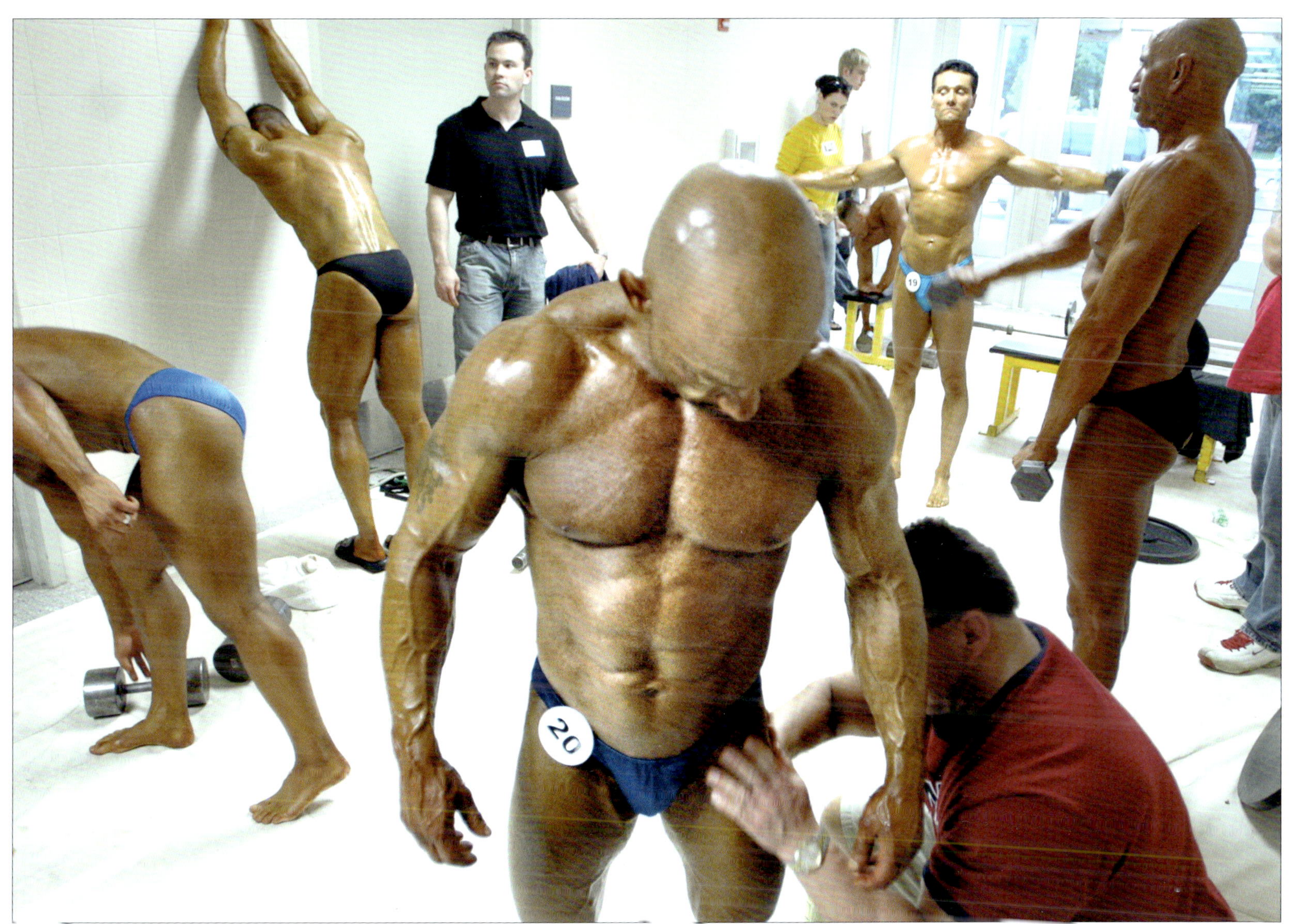
20
19

Jay Maynard, 44, is dressed as a character inspired by the movie *Tron* as he waits backstage during a costume contest at an annual science-fiction convention in Bloomington. "I'm wearing ten double A's and a 9-volt," said Maynard, who made his costume from spandex and electro-luminous wires.

"I've had about 15 radio interviews, three or four magazine stories. I have been on *Jimmy Kimmel Live* four times now, and there is at least one more segment in the can ready to run. I certainly didn't set out to do all that, but I thought, 'I'm on the tiger. I might as well grab his ears and enjoy the ride.'

Not all of the attention has been flattering. A couple online stories have drawn about a thousand comments, and only about 30 of them have been positive. Most of the rest were along the lines of: 'Fat guys in spandex don't look good' and 'My eyes will never be the same. Where's the bleach?' That really got to me. I was in Detroit after one story hit the Web and had to drive 12 hours alone with all those comments ringing in my head. It was like the eighth-grade class bullying the unpopular geek all over again.

In high school, I tried to do whatever it took to make that stop. I wanted to be one of the 'in crowd,' but I couldn't think of anything that I could do to change the fact that I wasn't. I've worked through all that now. I learned that if I don't accept myself, nobody will. But that doesn't mean it didn't still hurt. It hurt quite a lot. I wouldn't recommend anybody to spend hours on Interstate 80 after that kind of treatment."

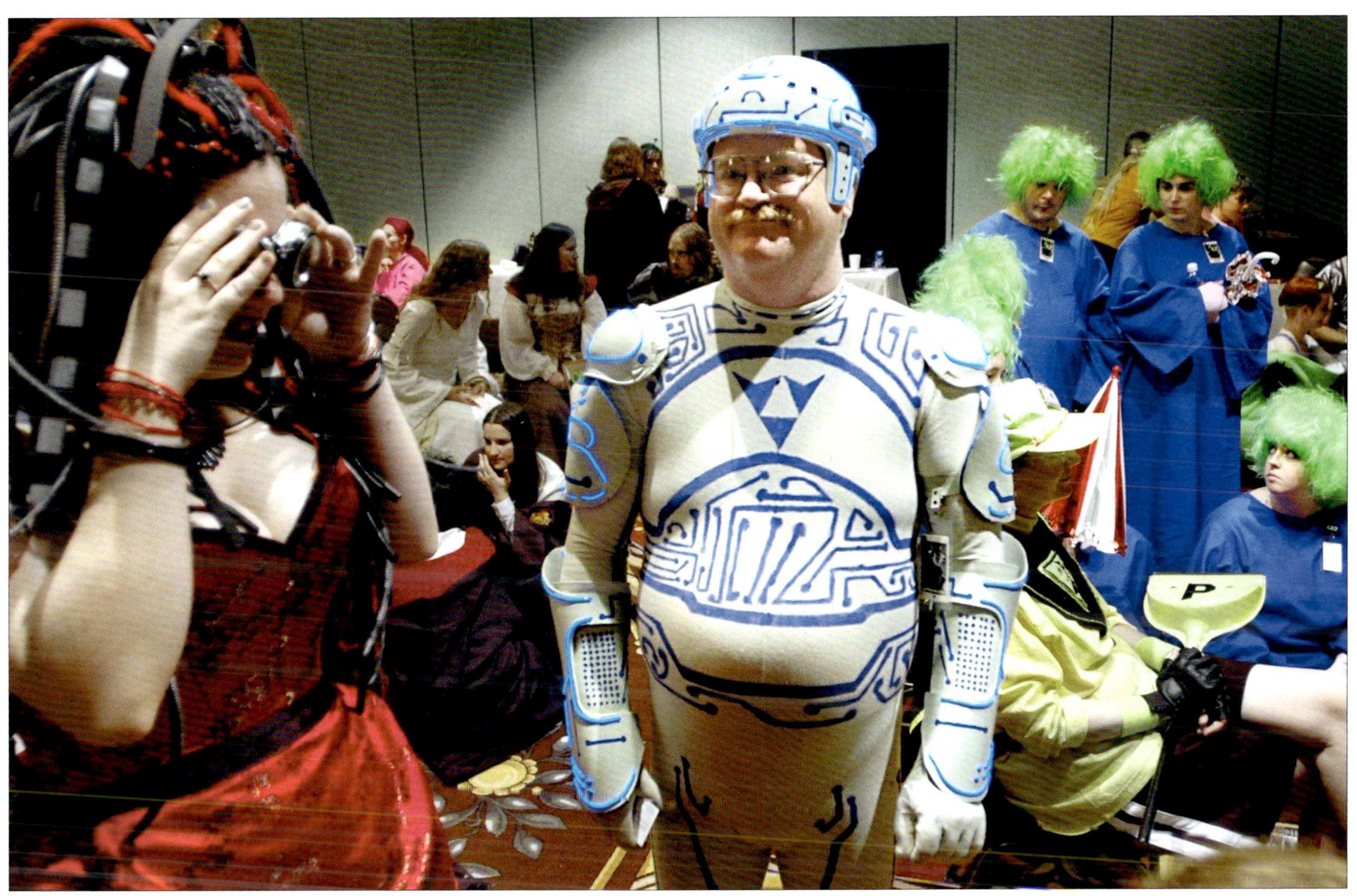
P

Former prostitute Doris Johnson, 42, right, tries to persuade an 18-year-old girl to come with her instead of a man she was with at a bus stop in St. Paul. Johnson works for Breaking Free, a social service agency that provides services and education to women and girls involved in prostitution.

"So I told her, I said, 'Well, you want to go with me right now? Go with me right now and you ain't never got to see him again.'

There's a part of her that wanted to go but, mind you, she's high right now. So she's figurin' in her mind, 'I'm gonna do this last one and that's it, I'm gonna go out with a bang.'

If I can get ahold of her, he can forget it. When you got somebody like me that's goin' to help you get out of there, that's goin' to make you feel safe and you feel that—that's a moment of clarity, and you want to stay in that moment.

Comin' from where I come from, I know that you don't have to stay out there, and if I can give somebody a hope shot, then that's what I'm going to do. Because it was given to me, and I'm giving it away—hope. Hope. That's what it's about. It's my job. My godly duty."

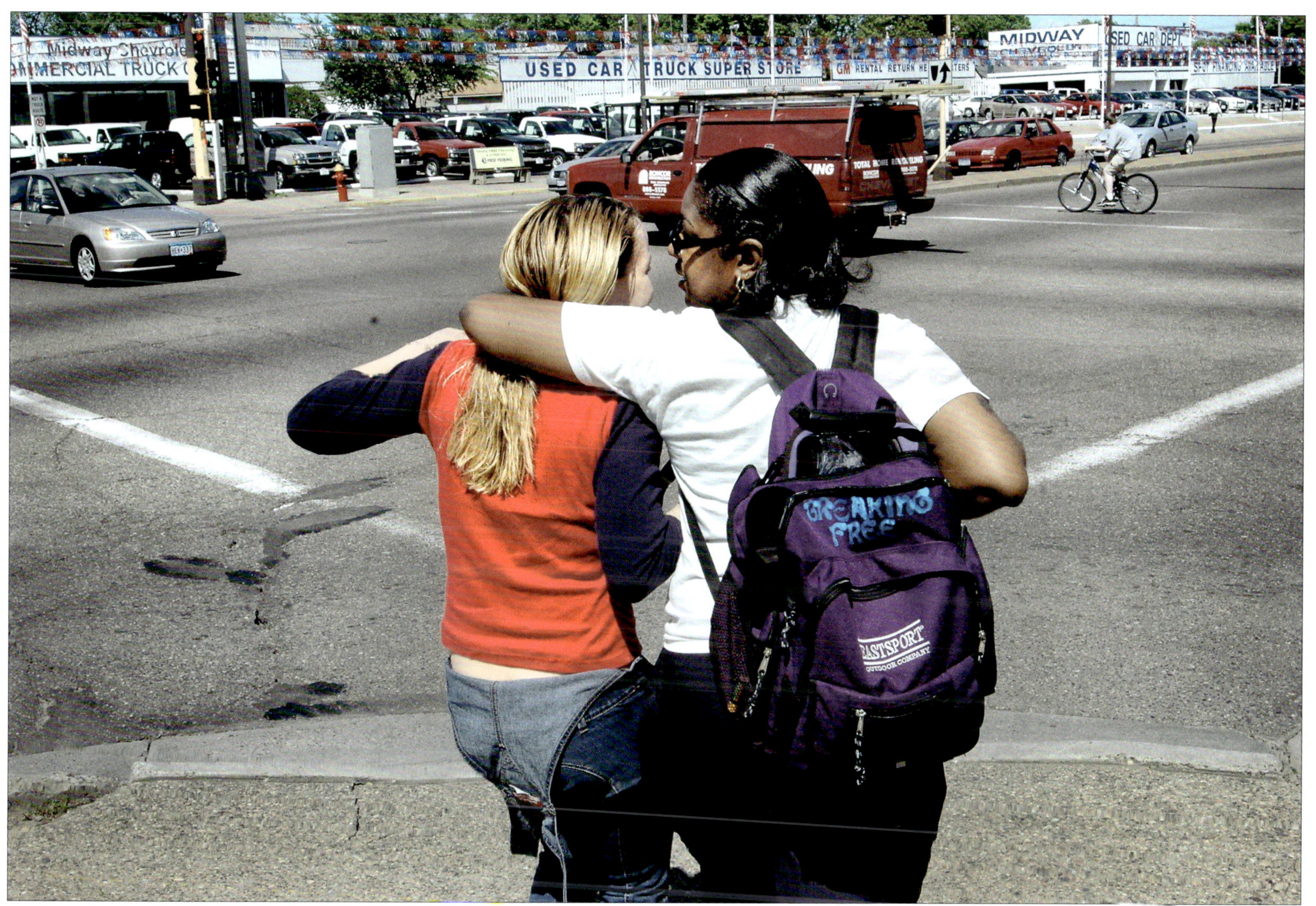
USED CAR TRUCK SUPER STORE
MIDWAY
USED CAR DEPT
EASTSPORT

Sister **Rose Hang Vu**, 55, collects aluminum cans from Pho Tau Bay, a Vietnamese restaurant in Minneapolis. She sells them and sends the money to the poor in her native Vietnam.

"In the beginning, for over ten years, I use the maintenance-man car. I get into the trouble because the cans are so smelly. Even I put air-freshener in the car, still I get into trouble. Finally, the sisters give me this old pickup truck. So I use it, and I collect the cans all around. With the smell, nobody else want to drive it.

Because I'm so small, the sisters tease me. 'Watch out for that pickup truck—there's no driver there!'

The first time I collect cans, I went to different parks; I went to the Vietnamese restaurant. I sold and got only $1.75. I was happy, but I was sad also, because for all my work, I got only $1.75. But I have enough for a few bowl of soups for the poor. Some people in Vietnam, the basic need is rice. I give them $2 for 10 kilo of rice. They are so happy to receive, even they cry."

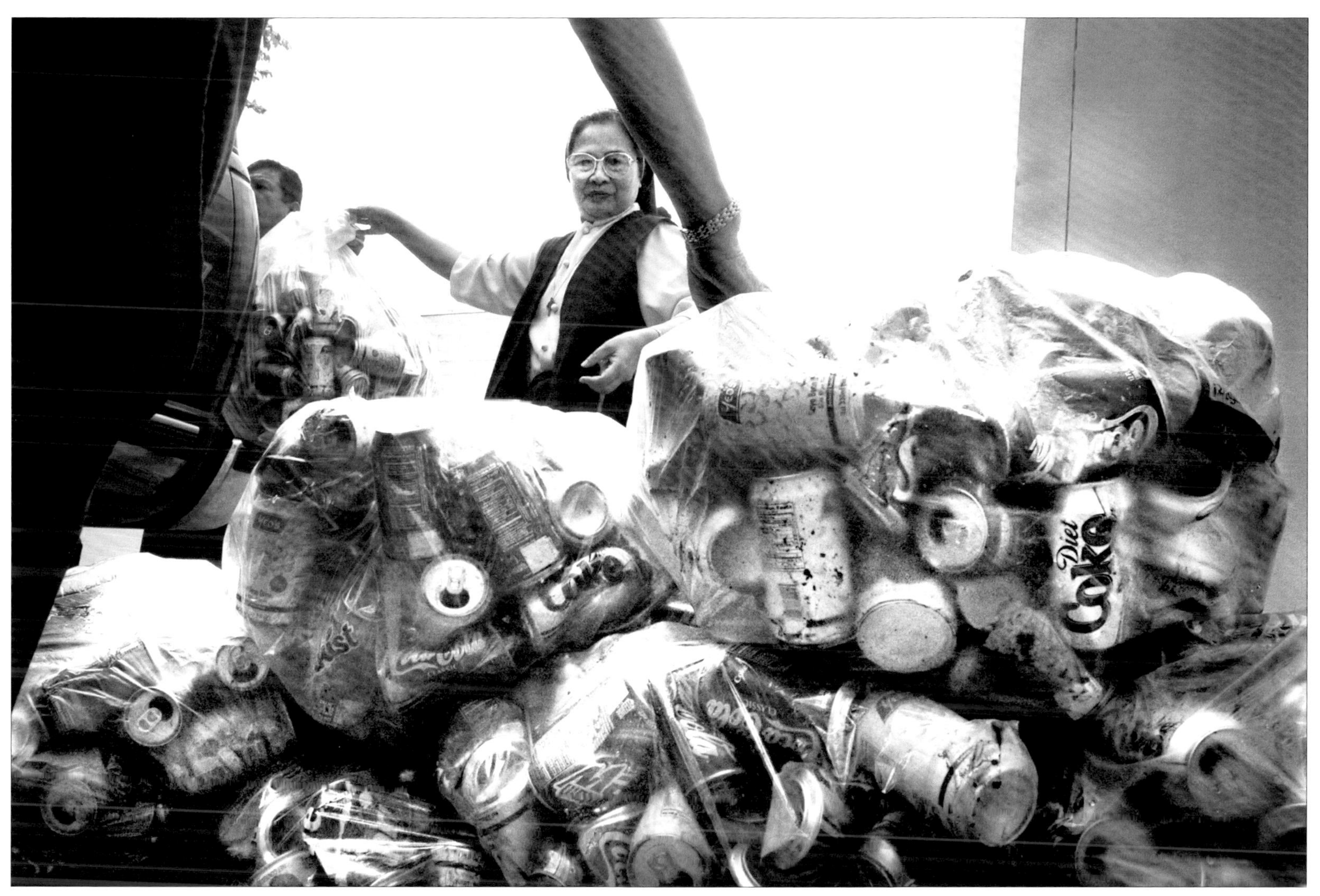
Diet
Coke

Ralph Elliot, 59, site director of Urban Academy Charter School in downtown St. Paul, comforts first-grader Lawrence Renfro after he felt teased by older students.

"I had a high school teacher, his name was Fred Gumbs. At that time, I guess I was trying to act a little thuggish, but I sang. I had a voice. He said, 'You know, you have a talent and could go somewhere, but you're too busy trying to be a thug. I won't let you ruin yourself.' He said, 'I will kick you so hard in your butt that every time you cough, a new shoe will pop out.' I says, 'You can't talk to me like that!' He says, 'I'm not supposed to, but I can, and I mean it. I won't let you go the wrong way.'

I think if more people were that way—more passionate, more involved, were not only inside their own little world but gave—we wouldn't have the problems that we have. There's not one of these kids that I won't put myself on the line for like that. 'Cause that's what it's all about. When you give, it comes back to you in a better society, a better city that you live in. So what do we lose?"

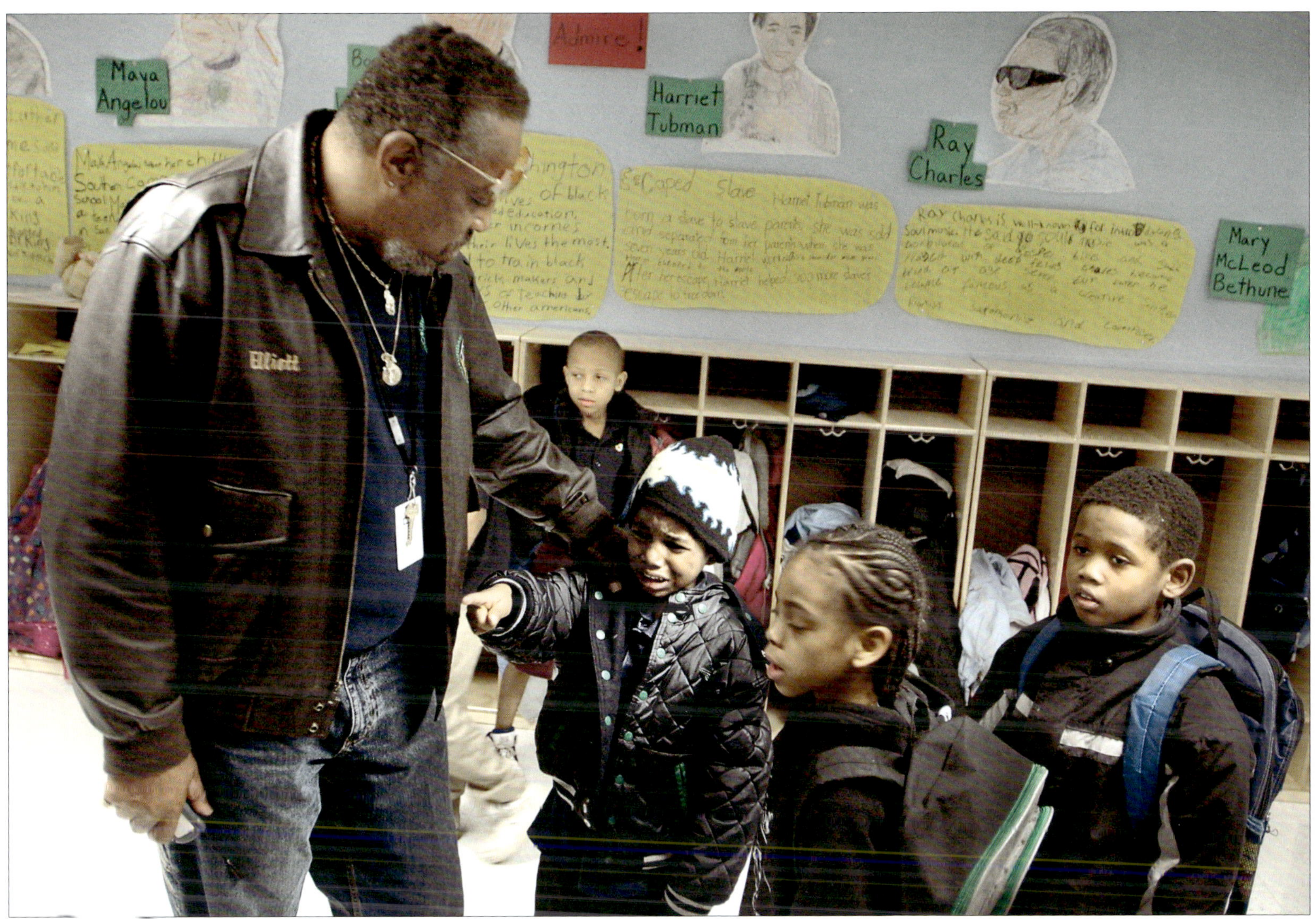
Admire!
Maya Angelou
Harriet Tubman
Ray Charles
Mary McLeod Bethune
Escaped Slave
Elliott

Bird Loiselle, 52, who has a rare degenerative condition called Buergers disease, rides his modified, three-wheeled motorcycle in Vadnais Heights.

"When I lost my first leg, it didn't affect me that much. I just went on with my life. When I lost the second one, that was drastic because then I was crawling around. Then I started losing fingers and hands, and I'm thinking, 'How am I going to work the throttle? How am I going to work the shifter?' I went for about nine years without riding.

But I'm real stubborn. I wasn't gonna let little things like losing my legs bother me.

I got together with a whole bunch of friends and we were able to figure it out. We used a master cylinder off a '65 Chev pickup for a brake that I activate with my thigh. Then, we built steering stabilizers. Now, I ride it 75 to 80 mph.

Riding it for the first time, it was like waking up from a coma. This year, I was able to go out to Sturgis with my friends. I was right in there, smelling the exhaust and grabbing the throttle like I used to. I was back again. That's what I told all them guys, 'I'm back in black!'"

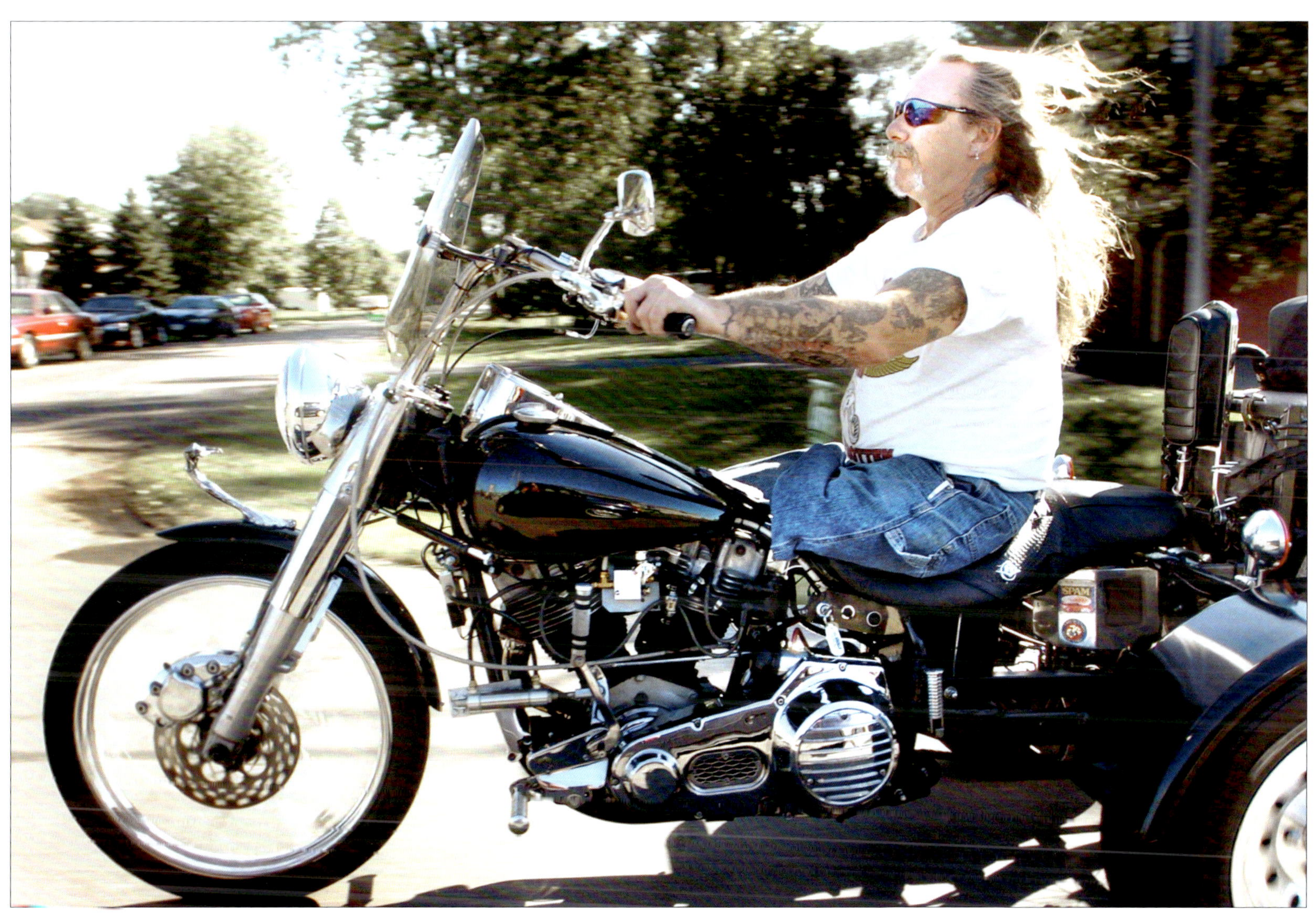
SPAM

Fomatta Dennis drives the streets of downtown St. Paul for the first time with a driving instructor. Dennis is from Liberia and is a senior at Concordia University.

"I thought it was going to be just in the parking lot, but then we went out, out on the highway!

I came home and told my husband, 'Guess what! Guess what! I drove on the highway!' He didn't believe me.

Then I called my mom. She didn't even believe that I did it. Then I called my sister in Africa. 'I drove on the highway! I went 60 miles per hour!' I called my best friend, too. Everybody couldn't believe that I did it.

I want to get my license. I can't wait. I have to take three buses to go to school. It's going to be a great help for my family, too. Right now, if my husband can't take us, we don't go. Every time I have to depend on somebody. Freedom, that is what I want."

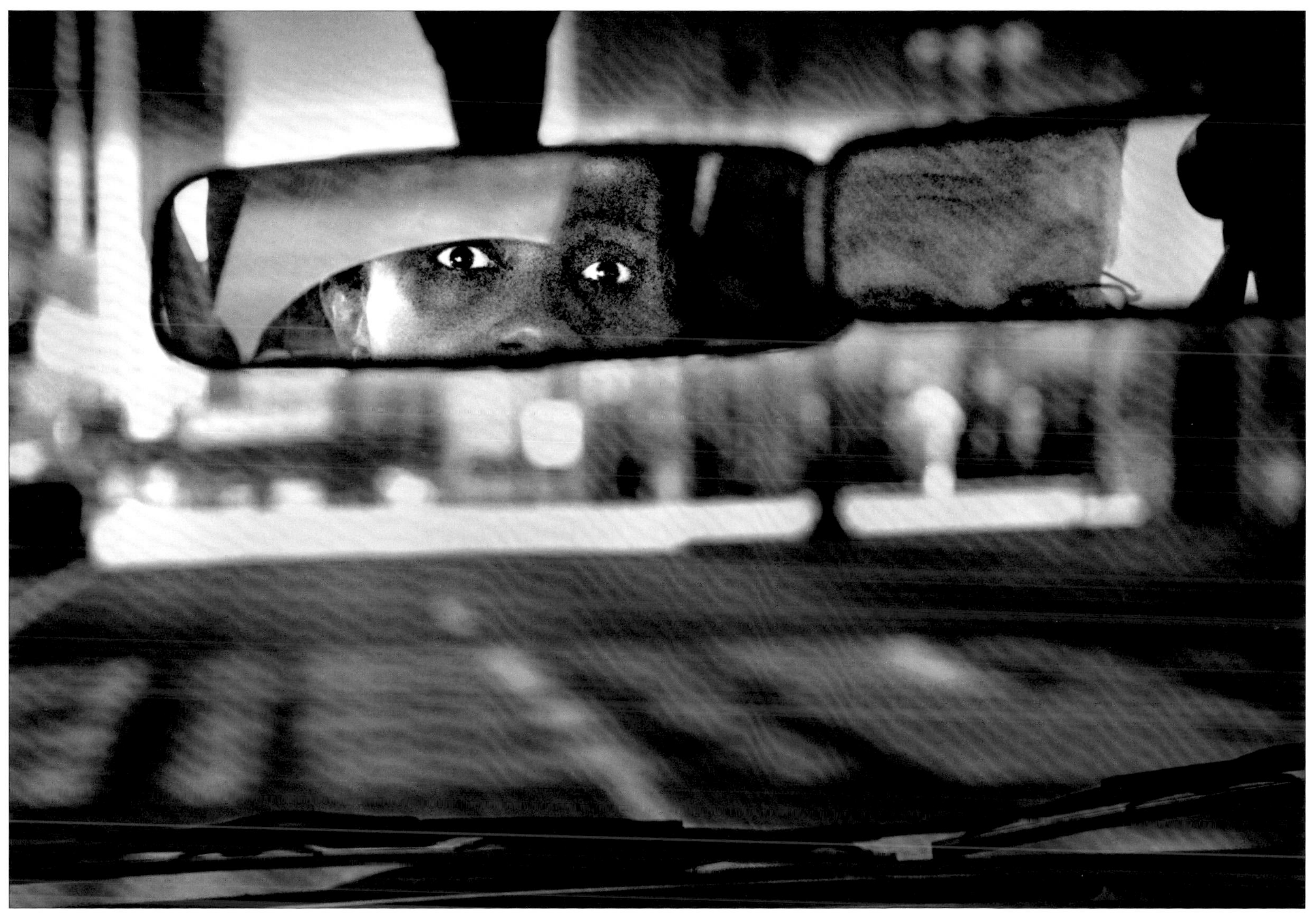

Eugene Harvey, 77 of Hugo, talks about his life.

"I worked at 3M for 37 years. We used to saw 4-inch asbestos sheets. Just had little paper masks and we didn't think nothing of it. It didn't hurt; it didn't itch, but it filled our lungs with asbestos. Now, nearly all the guys I worked with are dead and most of them died from cancer of the lungs.

The average doctor, he never labeled me as having asbestosis, but many years after I retired, I saw a specialist. It turned out that I sure did. I don't know how come others died, and I didn't. But I think mine is starting to kill me now. I'm getting very short of breath, and I got a lot of phlegm in my lungs. When I jump on my bike in the morning, I spit ten times between here and the post office.

I'm not afraid to die. I remember when I was a young guy I had my car in the shop for a flat tire. I'm waiting around for them to fix it, and some guy, not an old guy, in his 50s I guess, was waiting, too. I hear a noise, and I look around and all of a sudden he goes bloop. He fell right over and bounced a little. He was stone dead.

If I were to drop dead tomorrow, that's OK. Long as it ain't too miserable. That's the best way to go. Just walkin' around and go bloop."

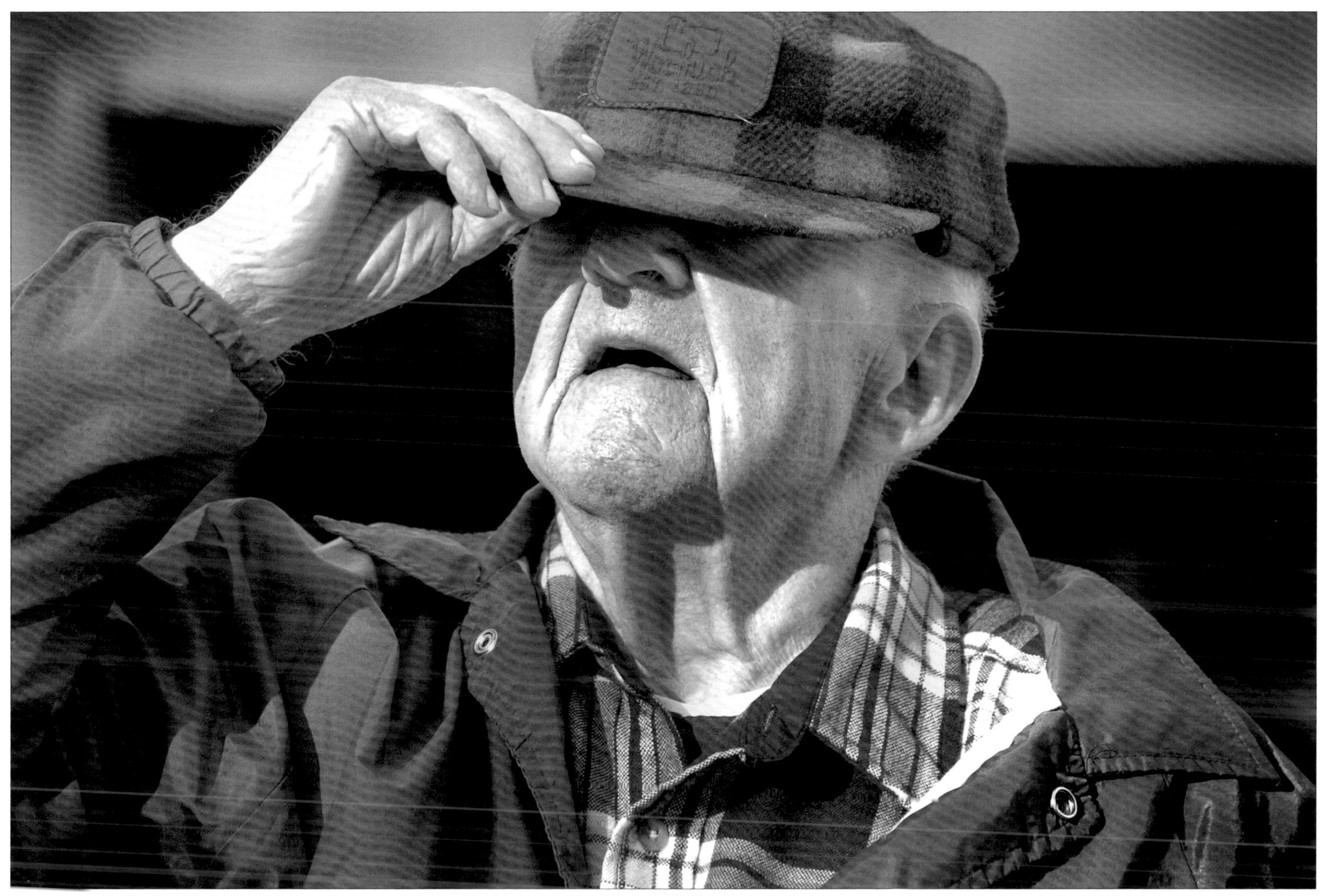

Mariachi singer Nacho Torres searches for the perfect hat at the Cinco de Mayo festival on St. Paul's west side. At right is his son Rey, 7.

"If I'm singing a romantic song I don't move too much. But if I'm singing a really happy song, I tend to dance, to do big moving. The hat has to feel just perfect. Not too tight, not too loose.

I think I take more time getting ready than my wife. My shower, my shaving, dressing up. When I was my son's age I wanted to dress up and couldn't. There was no money. I had a lot of young brothers. We were always tight, even on food.

My son, instead of asking me for toys, he asks me for another hat or another belt. "How come you have a big huge mariachi sombrero and I don't?" When he started walking he put his little feet in my big boots. He always wants to wear exactly like me. He's proud of me and his Mexican culture. I can see in the way he talks to me, the way he looks. He makes me so proud."

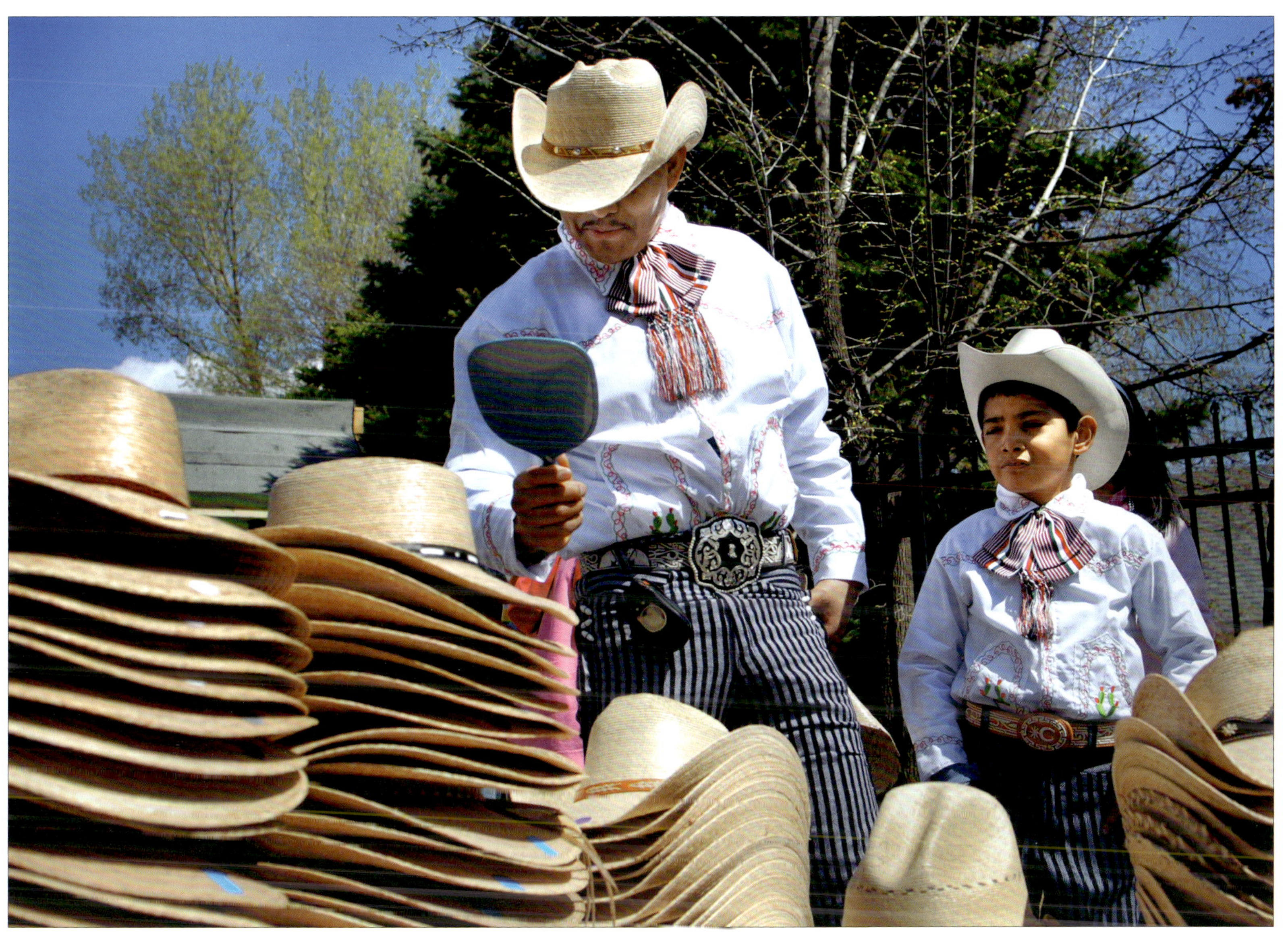

Chris Droen, 30, polishes metal parts
on the factory floor at Thorud Inc., in Bloomington.

"Sometimes I feel like a robot, like a drone. I go to work every day, punch the clock, work all day long and punch out. I do the same thing day after day. I worry that my brain might turn to mush.

If I was to do it over again, I might go with another type of machining career or something totally different, like heating, venting or air conditioning. Something hands-on and that might have a possibility of making more money. And maybe not quite so dirty, you know? Sometimes I worry about the stuff in the air."

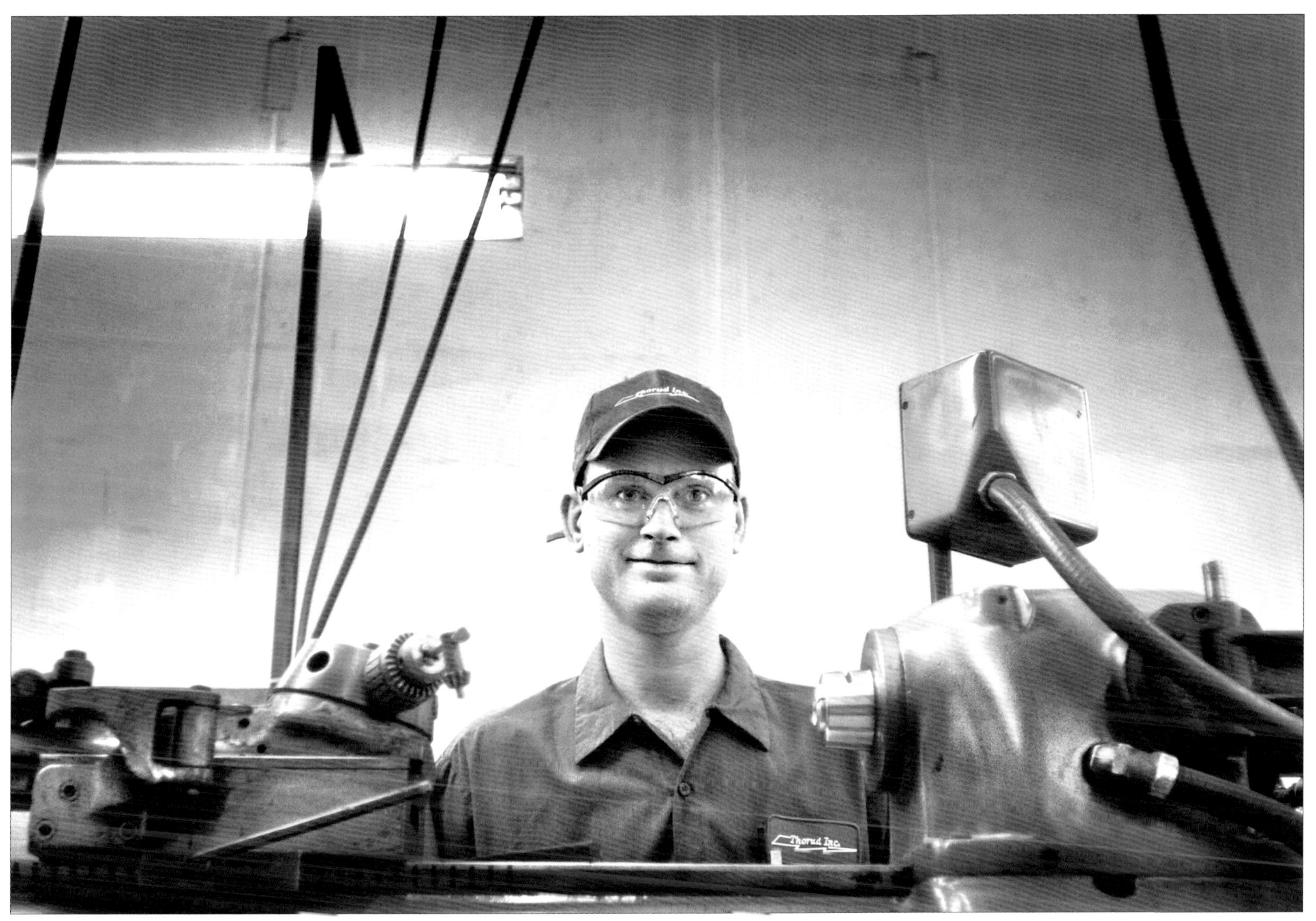
Thorud Inc.

Aimee Lor, 35, holds her two-month-old daughter, Pakujai, as friends and family tie white yarn around their wrists as a way of wishing the family health and happiness. More than 150 people were at the Hmong blessing ceremony in St. Paul to welcome the baby into the family.

"My husband and I had been trying for two years. It would have cost $15,000 for in vitro fertilization. We don't have a whole lot of money, so I said, 'Let's try the herbalist. A shaman.' The shaman is like a priest. She will try to get the evil spirits away. Hmong women, if they can't get pregnant, believe that evil spirits destroy their egg at the beginning of the month.

She gavc us some herbs—I drank them and my husband, he ate them. She said my uterus was too low so she repositioned it. She used her hands on my belly and just kind of pushed it up. I was amazed.

We hired her around June and I got pregnant in August.

We were so glad everybody was there at the blessing ceremony, to see their faces. We sacrificed a cow to welcome the baby to the family. Now as a mother I feel, I don't know … I just feel so blessed."

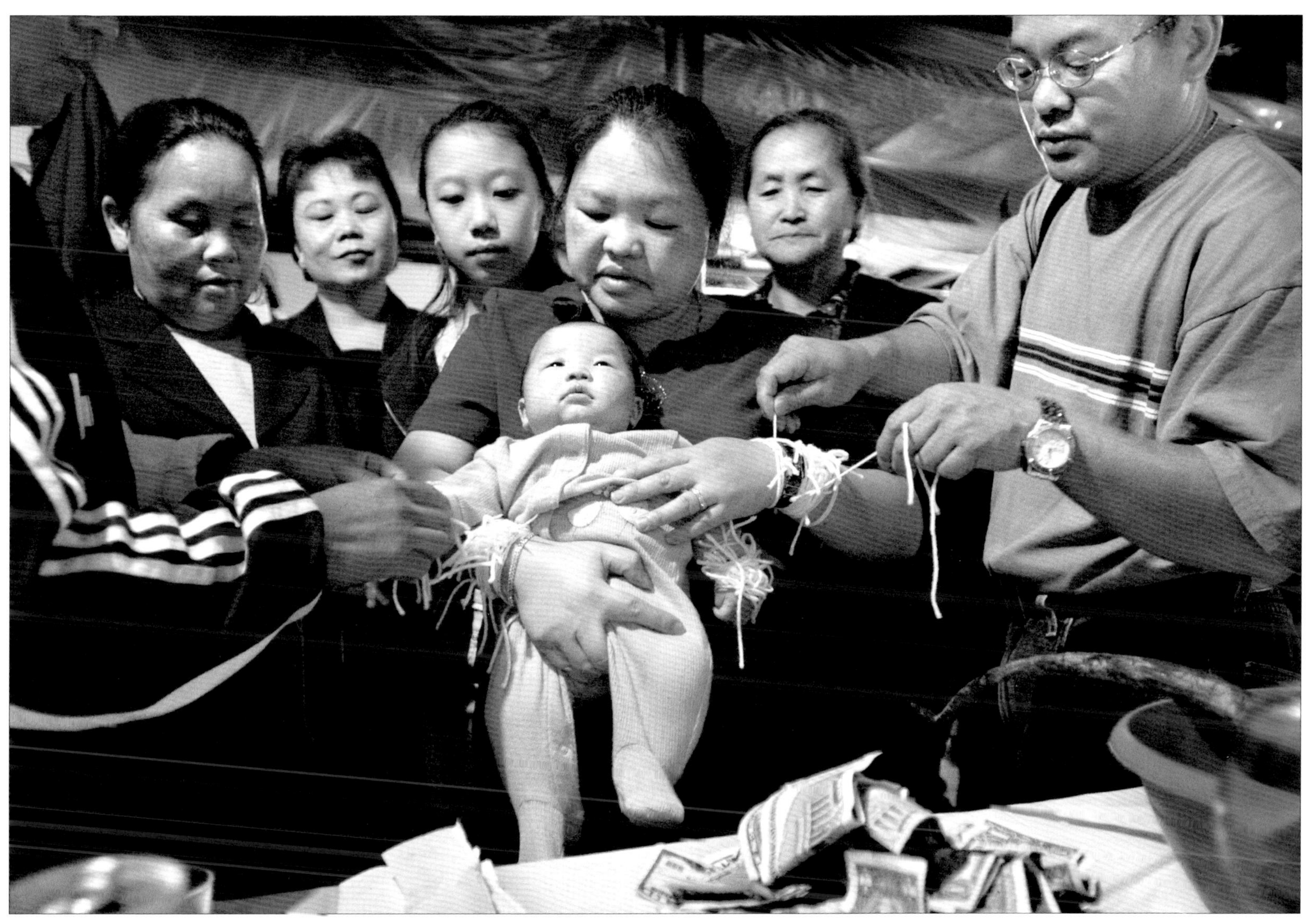

Twenty-three-year-old Francis Bonaldo of Montreal receives an acupuncture treatment at the American Academy of Acupuncture and Oriental Medicine in Roseville. He's a student at the school and is studying to become an herbalist.

"Canada is a less stressful place. People walk around more, have lunch for longer. At home, we just sit for an hour or two and watch the river flow. If we didn't have that, just doing nothing, relaxing, something would be wrong.

People here feel so guilty. I've heard people say, 'Oh, I'm not putting enough into my company,' or 'I'm not working enough.' The army, the war, the orange or red code or whatever. Which level of stress should you have today? In Canada, I don't even know what the army looks like. I just don't think about stuff like that. I think about life, living, day to day. Here it's 'What if this happens?'"

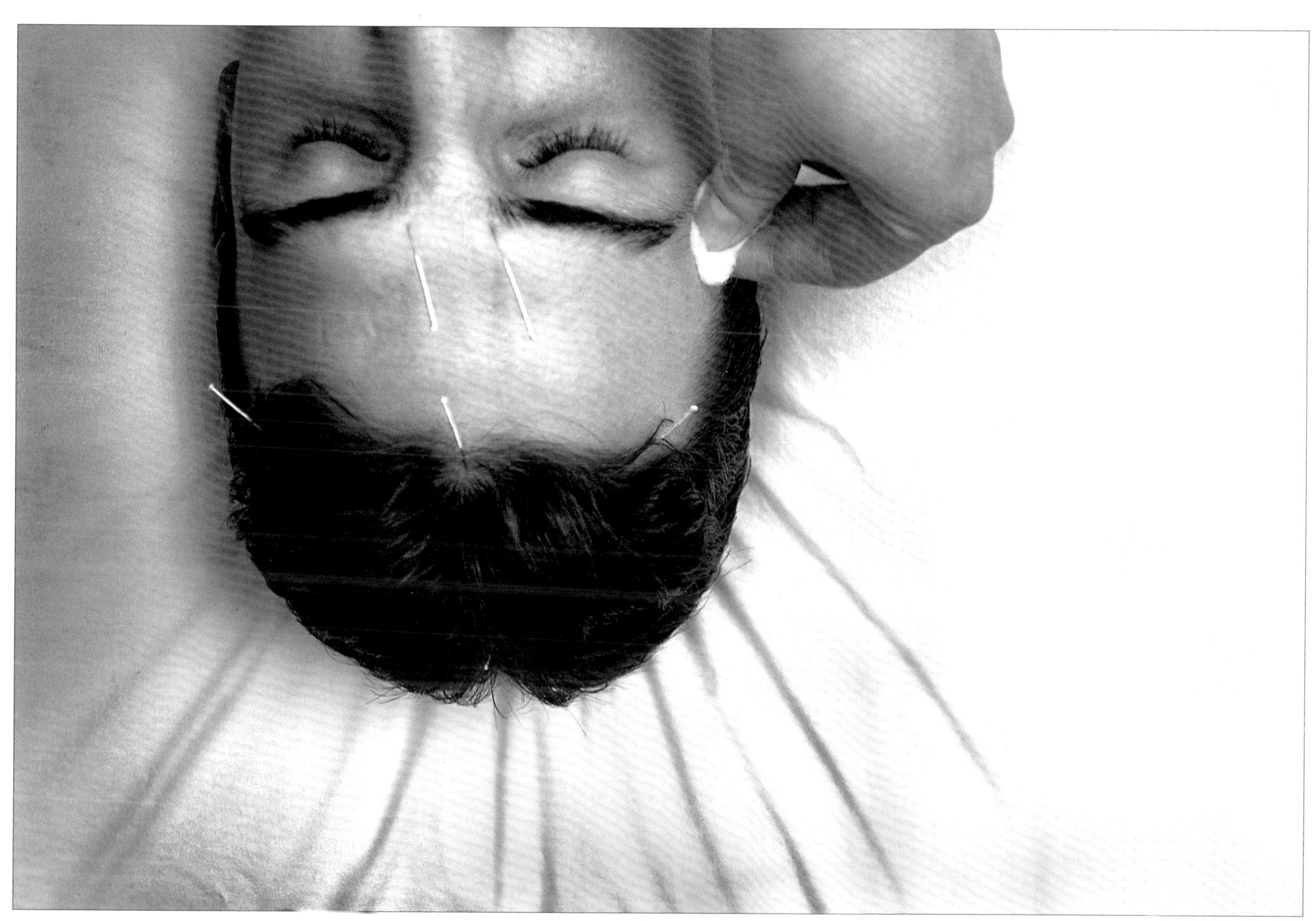

Backstage at the Quest nightclub in Minneapolis, 16-year-old Liz Kammerer tries to remain calm moments before walking the runway in a fashion show.

"It's nice to have people actually look at me. It makes me feel so much better about myself. During the show, I did two poses at the end of the runway, and people were just screaming and hollering and yelling and whistling. I kept a straight face the whole time.

When you're a teenager, you always get these magazines in the mail, and there are these models that are always looking pretty. They have perfect bodies. I see them and think, 'I want to be a model just like them.' That's what I want, for people to see me and say, 'I want to be just like her.' I want to get noticed by a lot more people, to get attention from them and feel like I actually did something."

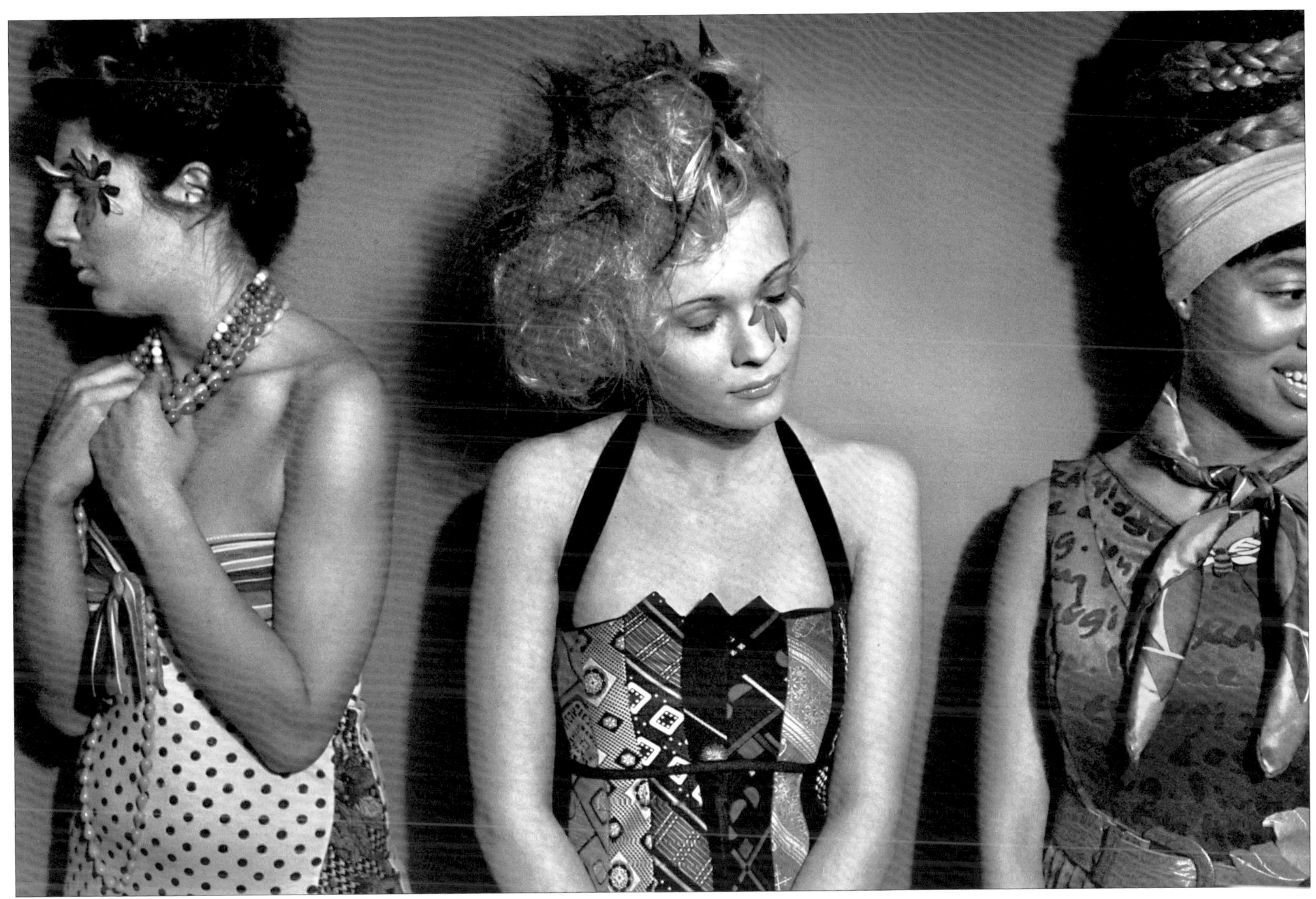

Five-year-old Alita Todd faces the audience after handing a trophy to 19-month-old Haley Shegstad during a "Most Beautiful Baby" contest at Rosedale Mall in Roseville. Alita and her mother, Anita, travel throughout Minnesota to compete.

"With Alita winning the second top prize at state last year, we have to go out and represent. She hands out trophies and the crowns and stuff for the new regional winners. It kind of goes with the crown, just like Miss Minnesota, Miss America. It's part of her obligation. Our obligation.

Right now, I'm getting ready for state. They have several different categories. You have to buy sportswear, swimwear, pajama wear, play wear, western wear, then the formal gown. I enjoy doing all the little dress-up and picking out her outfits. If she wins in a category, she not only won, but I won, too. It's like she's my finished product."

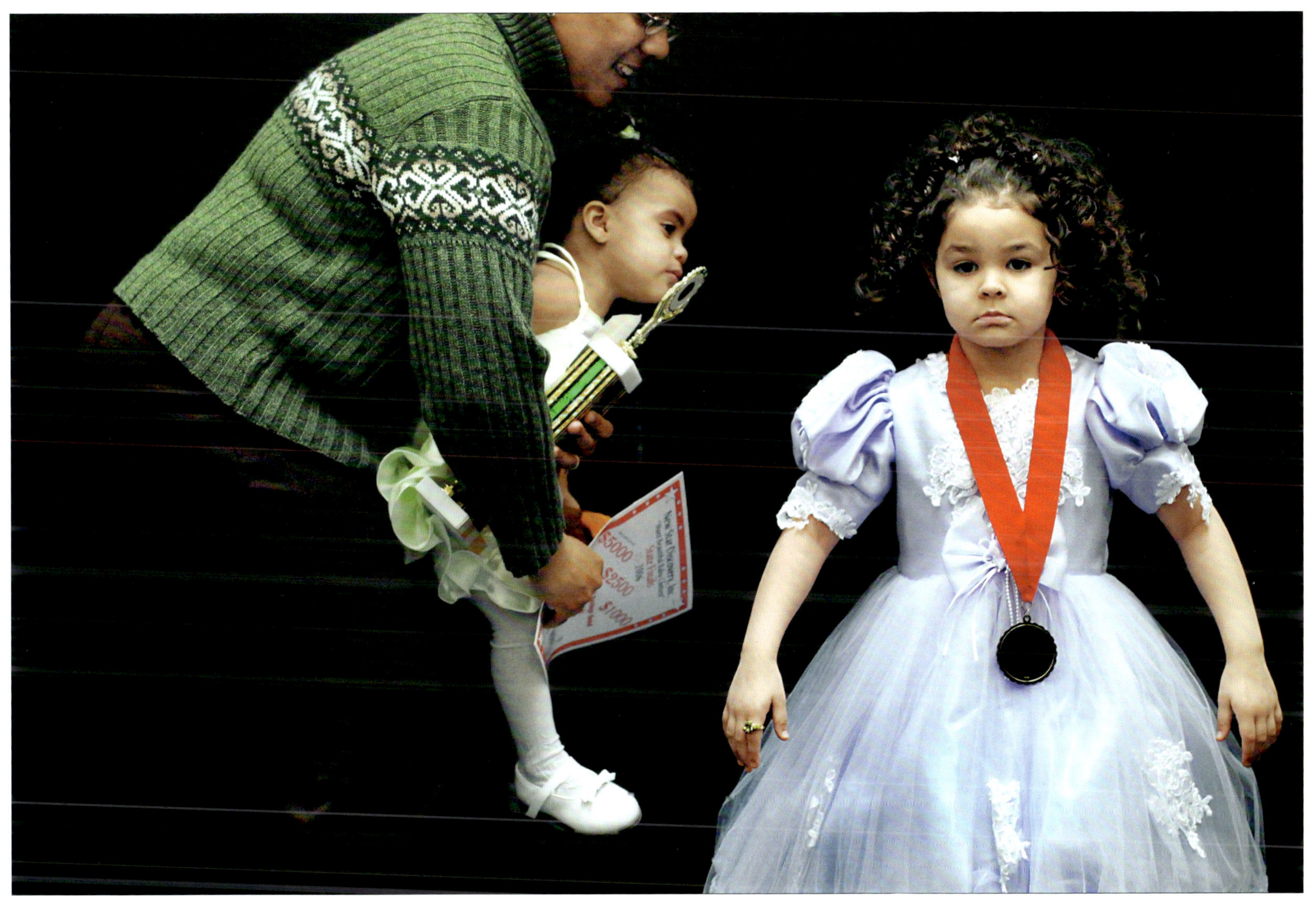

New Star Discovery, Inc.
State Finals
$5000
$2500
$1000

Richard Hunt, 49, left, shakes Jim Snook's hand
to close the deal on his new $60,000 Hummer in Roseville.

"It's just a big, solid, massive vehicle. You feel like you're in an armored car. I don't know if that's quite the words to use, but it feels like you should be part of the presidential entourage, you know?

I haven't really paid much attention to the gas mileage, but I think it averages about 8 or 9 miles per gallon, which is what my Escalade gets. It doesn't bother me whether I get 8 miles or 4 miles or 10 miles. It's secondary to the enjoyment that I get out of the vehicle.

It's cream of the crop. It's top of the line. I don't want to sound like I'm boasting or anything. I'm just a regular, average guy who appreciates quality and nice things. And, of course, my son had some influence on it, too. He's a teenager, and, you know, they all just go nuts over Hummers and Escalades."

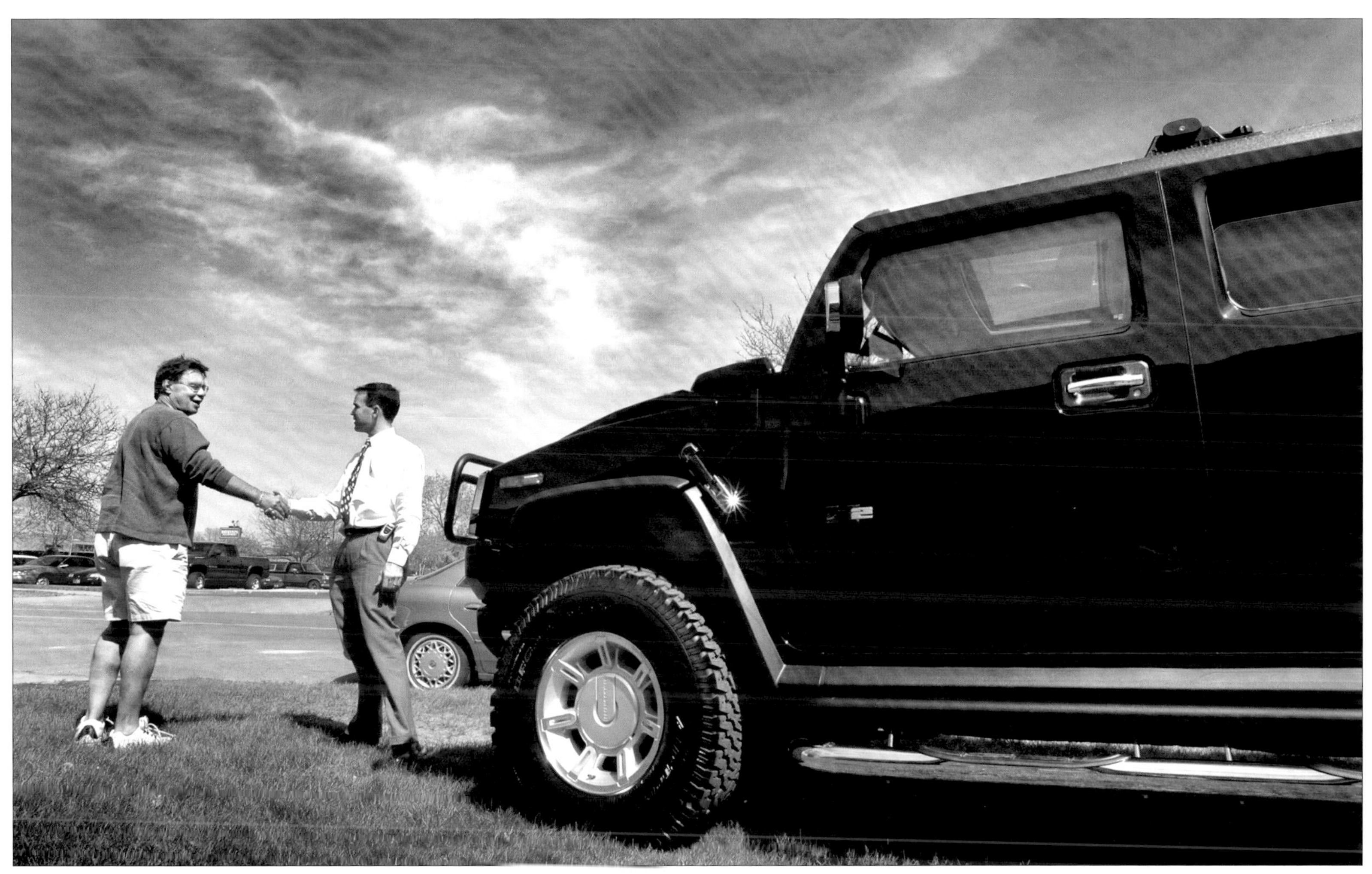

Siblings Kacy West, 19, left, and Keon West, 21, salsa dance at a late-night dance party in St. Paul. From Jamaica, they are in Minnesota to study at Macalester College. Keon, a Rhodes scholar, studies psychology and French. Kacy studies Spanish and political science.

Keon: Americans make apple pies, French people drink, and Jamaicans dance. It's just something that everybody knows how to do. Amongst your friends, if you can't dance, you have a problem.

Kacy: Not only dancing, but good dancing.

Keon: We started salsa five years ago. Kacy's actually one of my favorite dance partners.

Kacy: You're one of mine, too. But if we weren't related, we probably could do other moves … you know, sexier kind of moves. But we can't. That's the only limit. Keon is a good lead because you know exactly what he wants you to do and where he wants you to move.

Keon: I'm very deliberate about, 'You will spin now. And now you will stop spinning.' But I never hurt the person I dance with.

Kacy: Well, I don't go that far.

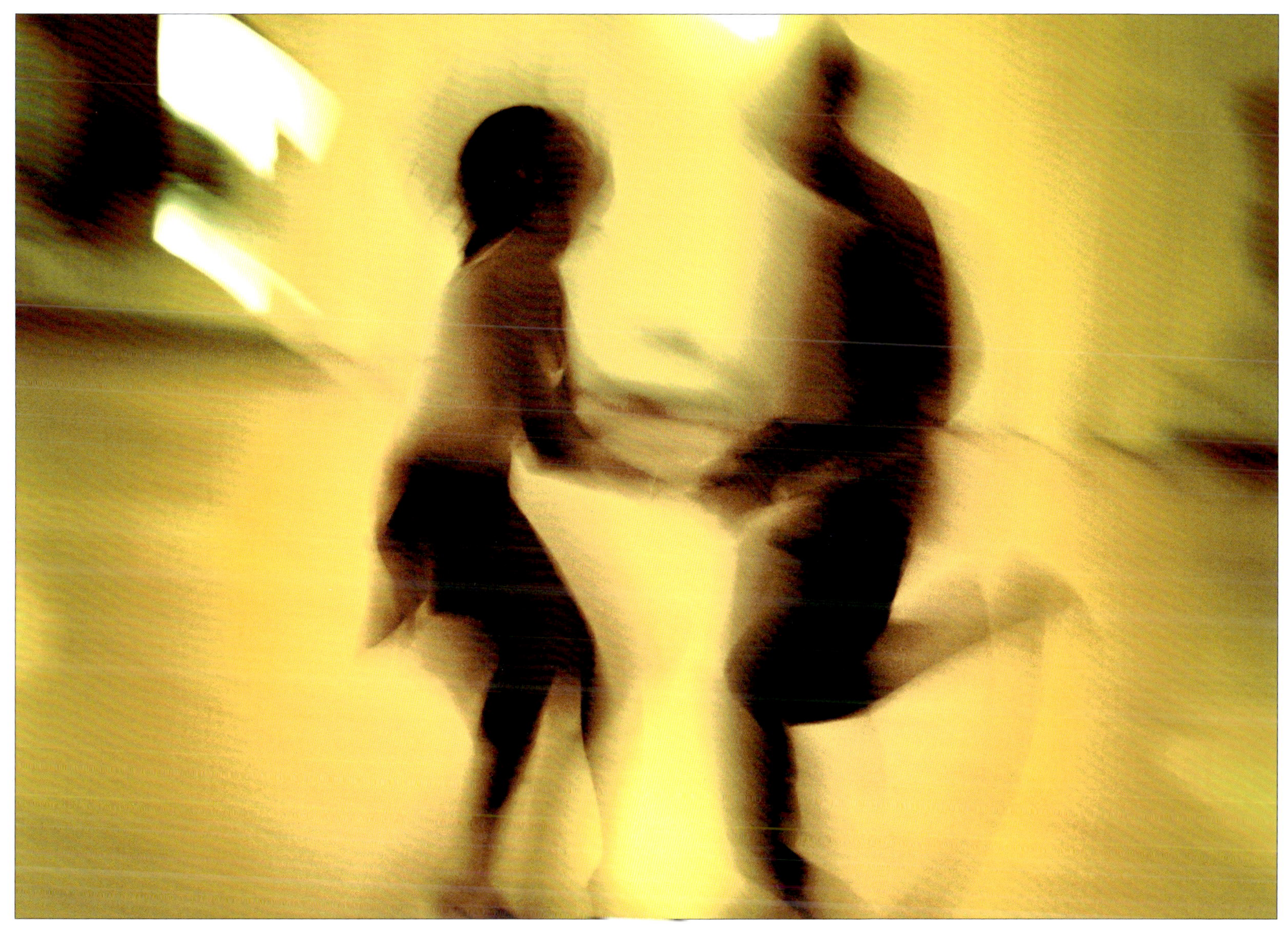

Jim Kemp, 72, of Minneapolis, dances with Rod King, 32, at the North Star Regional Gay Rodeo in Hugo. Kemp, who was married for 29 years, came out as a gay man 15 years ago.

"I have two daughters and one granddaughter. They love me dearly, and we're very close. A lot of gay fathers aren't that fortunate. That was one of the hardest things for me when I came out, hearing the horror stories of what wives and churches did to some fathers. It's just unbelievable.

One man from South Minneapolis came home from work one afternoon and the elders of the church were on the front step. They had two bags packed with clothes and said, 'You're not going in the house. You will never speak to your family or three kids again or they'll all go to hell, just like you.' And now, 15 years later, he's gotten word he has grandchildren. He asked, 'Can I at least have a picture of my kids?' 'Absolutely not.' He had to just walk away from that house and never go back. Stories like that, they go on and on.

But it's changed in the last 15 years so much. When I first came out, I never dreamed I'd be caught on the streets of Minneapolis holding a guy's hand, and, of course, today I don't think anything about it. There's a great sense of freedom now, to be able to hold hands or to dance like we're dancing."

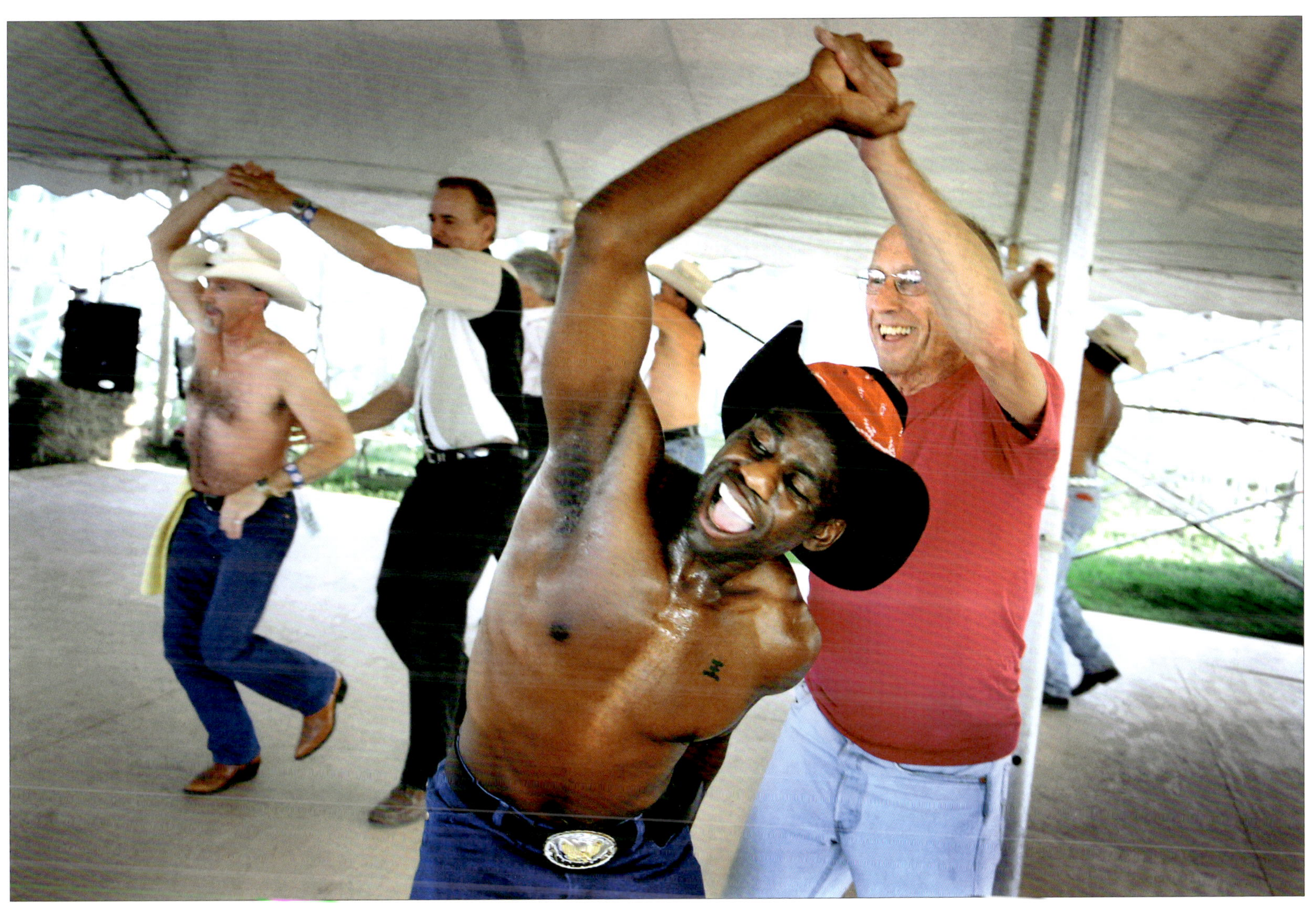

Peter Martin, 45, plays a 1976 "Team One" Gottlieb pinball machine in his dining room in Shafer. He collects and repairs old pinball machines.

"When I push a button to start a machine, it creates this mechanical music. I hear that clicking and the solenoids functioning and I can picture all the systems and how they work. I have to know how they work. I just *have* to. I want to live it, I want to breathe it, I want to experience it for what it is completely. Even if it's just a pinball machine.

I do lots of things for people, and then once in a while I like the rules to be broke for me. I can have ten machines inside my house right in my living room. That's probably why I'm single; I do things that take a lot of extra understanding."

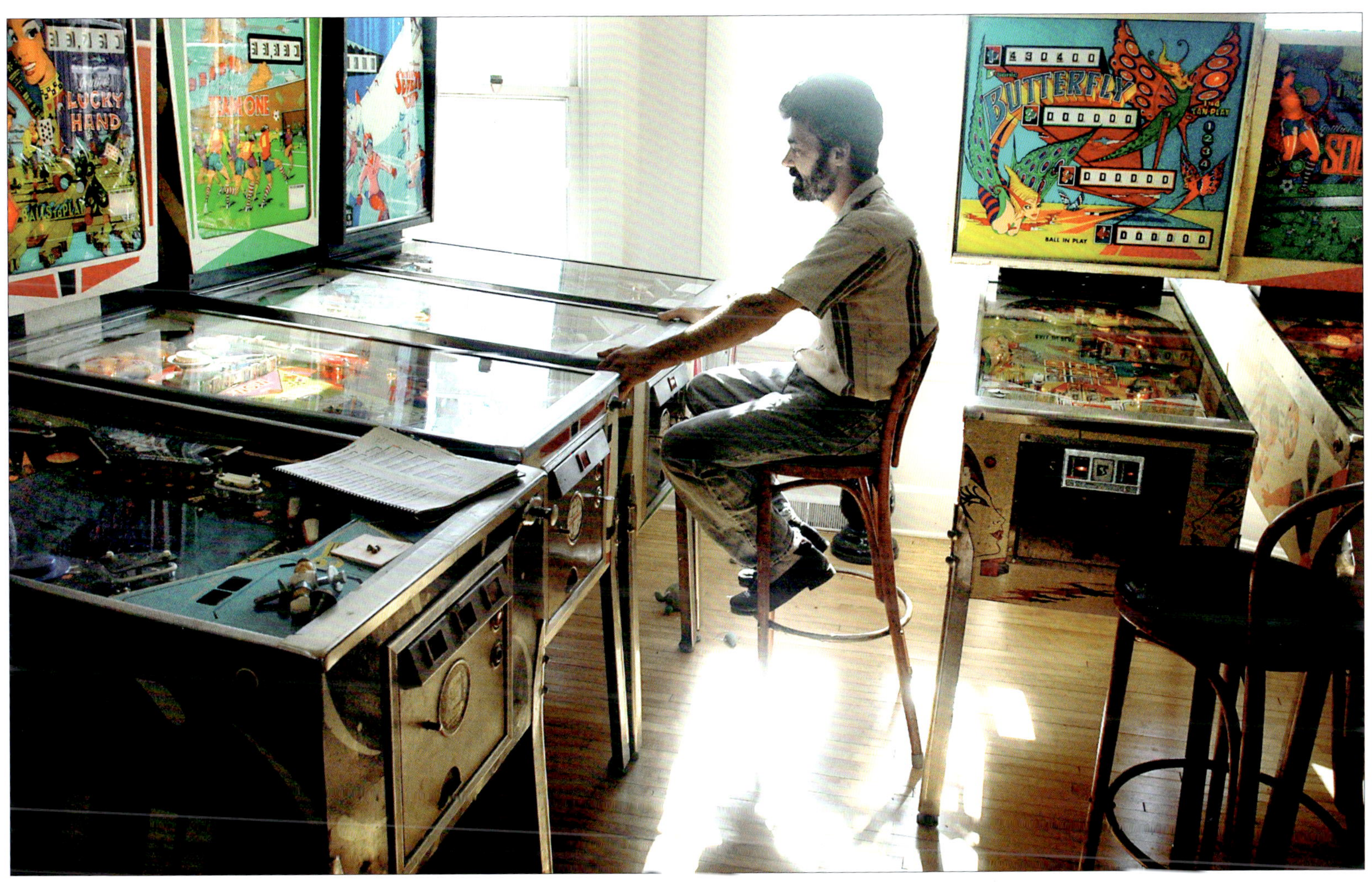
LUCKY HAND
BUTTERFLY

Seventeen-year-old Kayla Schiltgen walks with a boar after feeding the animals at her family's farm in Hugo.

"My sister said that someday I'm going to start the 'Don't Let Any Fly Die Club' because I'm always so friendly and gentle with animals. I think I'd be the nicest vet. I'd take the best care of animals and would always be really gentle. I've given shots and done ear notching and teeth clipping and tail clipping. I know that's just minimal, but I don't mind doing that. I actually enjoy it.

I've never really been a religious person, but I believe that we were all put on the earth at the same time, and God wanted all of us to be treated the same. He says that we should love one another, but he never specifies who 'one another' is. 'One another' could be animals or humans, or basically everything like plants and animals and trees and the environment."

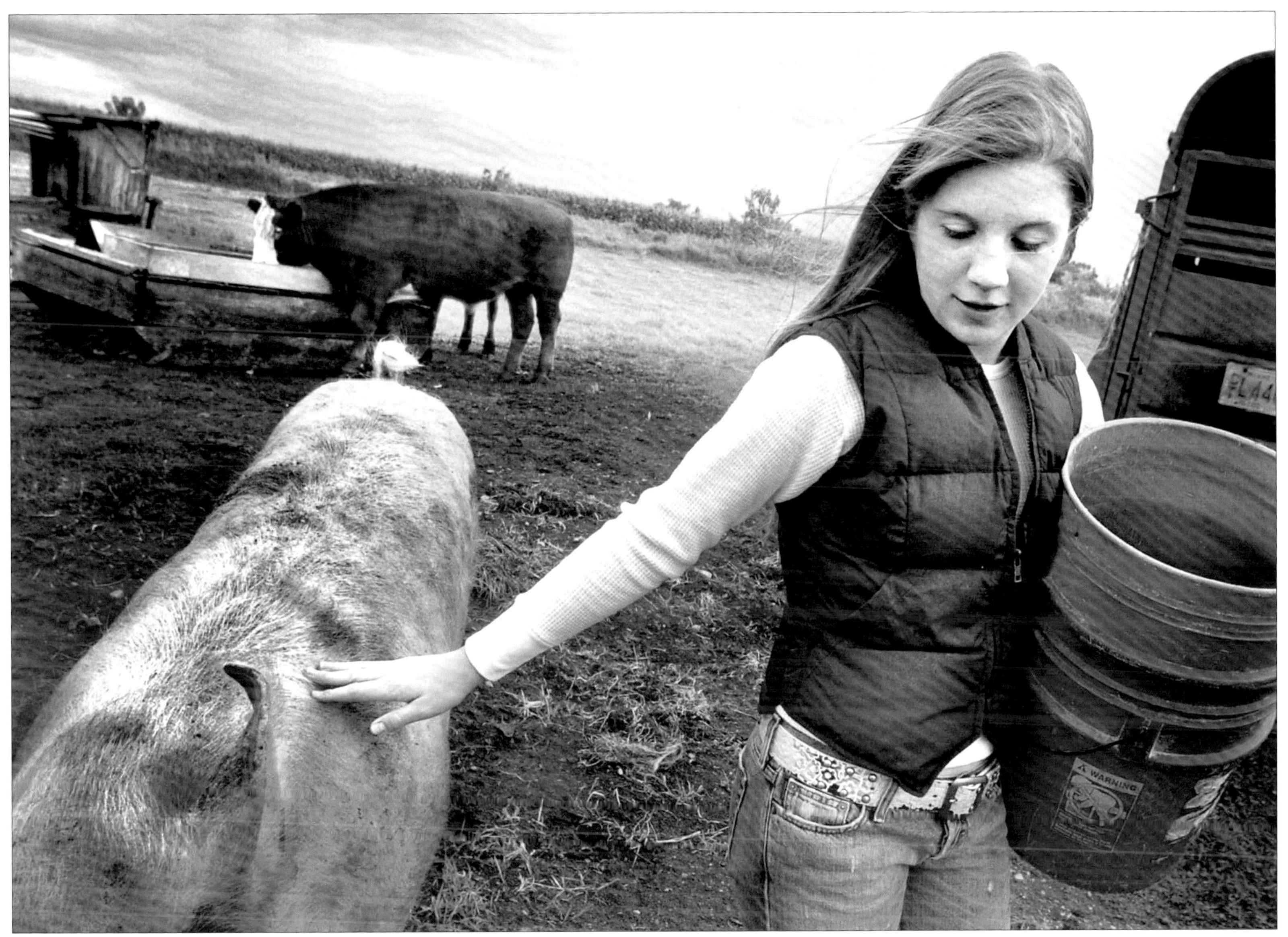
WARNING

Bill Seed, 45, holds his pug, Maddie,
after she was awarded first place in the annual "Pug O' Ween"
costume contest at a pet store in Shoreview.

"She's a mutant pug mummy. Getting her to sit still and wrap about 20 yards of gauze around her was quite a process, as you can imagine.

The idea of making her into a tarantula just got to be too complicated, although she would have made a really great tarantula.

I have just never seen so many pugs in one place at one time. There are butterflies and ballerinas and ducks and pigs. This is chaos, insanity, hysteria, and this is absolute and utter joy. When you look at them, you can't help but laugh.

I live with chronic depression, and I come home every day and there's this absolutely ridiculous face, looking at me, begging for attention and asking for love. And who can resist that?"

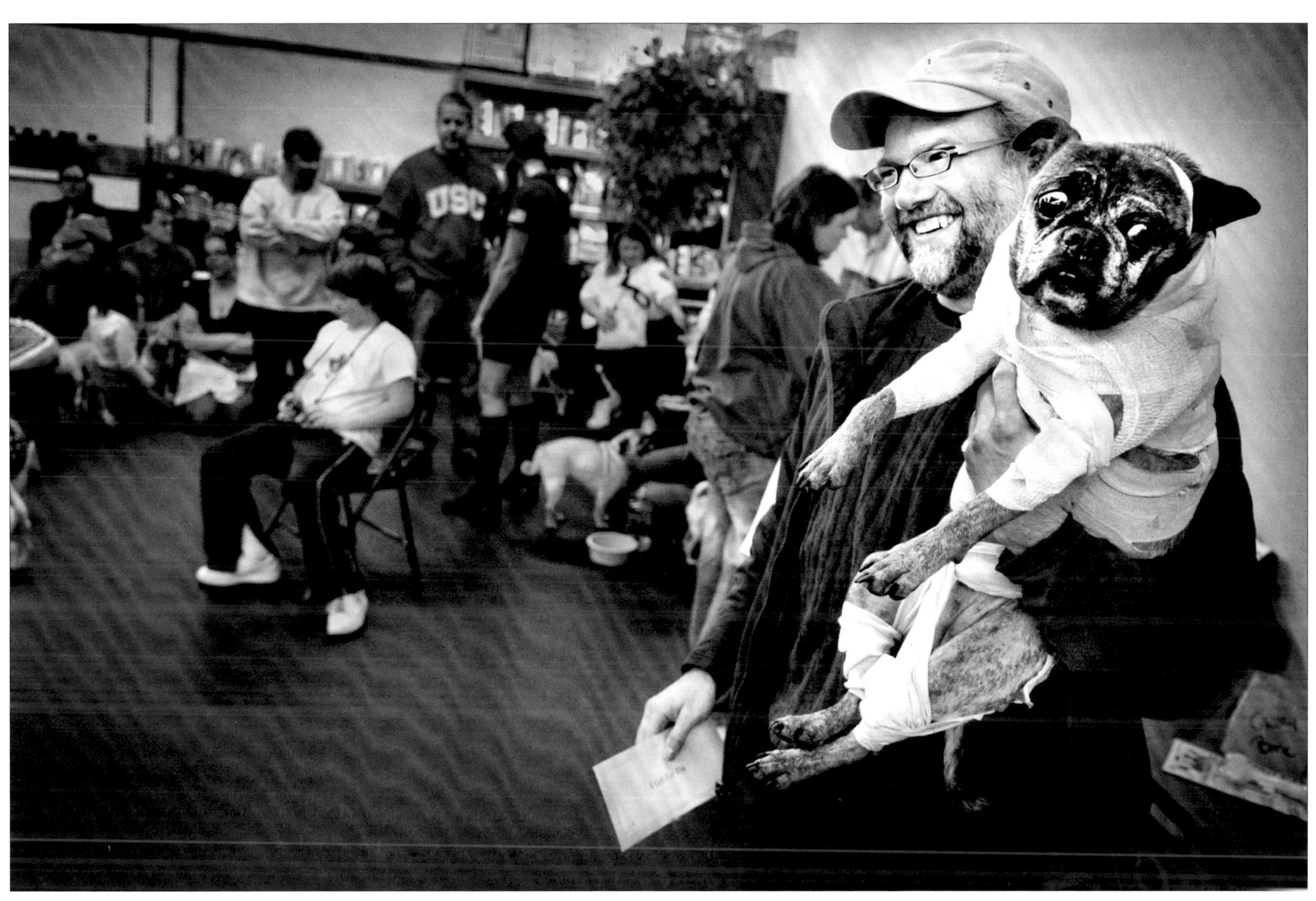
USC

Jake Reynolds, 32, comforts his nine-year-old son Hassan after he crashed his bike in Minneapolis. Reynolds was released from prison recently after serving seven years for forging cashiers' checks as part of a cross-country counterfeiting ring. He now lives in St. Paul and visits his son and seven-year-old daughter Lailah twice a week.

"When I got out of prison their mom called me and said, 'You know, I told the kids you're home and they want to see you.' I was walking up to the door and thinking about all of the things that I wanted to say, that I have been wanting to say for seven years. But I couldn't think of anything. I just knocked on the door and opened it up.

My son, he rushed to me, he jumped into my arms: 'Daddy, Daddy.' My daughter just kind of sat back. She had never even seen me before. I came in and sat down next to her and just, I just stayed quiet. I didn't look her directly in the eyes; I didn't know what to say to her. I think she was afraid of who I was or who I was going to be. All she had seen were these pictures of me in a prison uniform, big and mean looking, a scary guy. Then, when she saw that I wasn't like that in person, I don't know, she was able to open up to me. Now her and I have just an incredible, incredible relationship.

My son, on the other hand, he had fabricated this image of me as this perfect dad. When I come home everything was going to be all right. Then Daddy came home and I'm not a perfect dad. I don't know how to be. It almost seemed like he was just crushed. I don't know. My goal now is to just do the best I can dofor him, whether it is time or trust or some sort of … I don't know what the word is, consistency?"

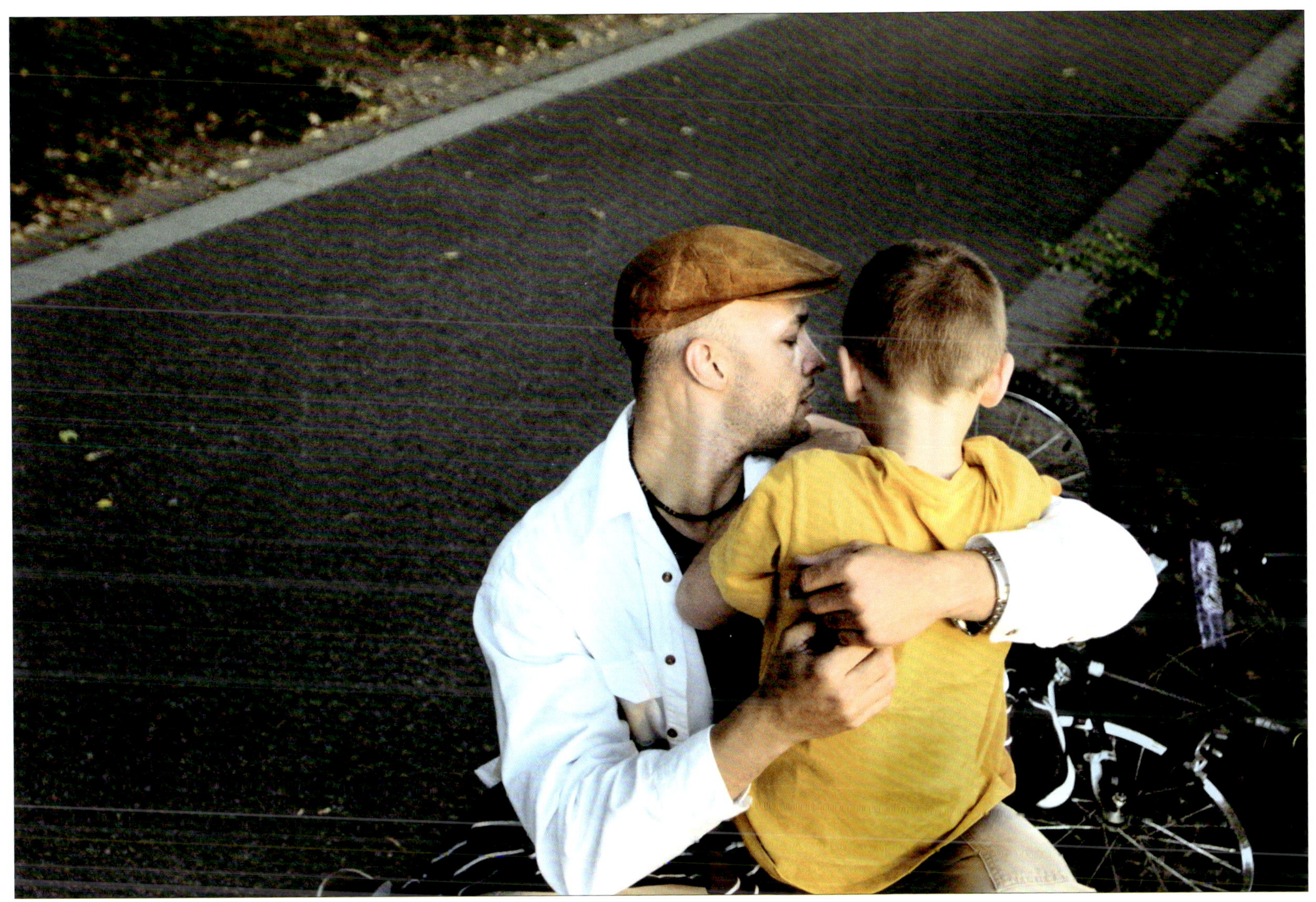

Second cousins John Broecker, left, 79, and Dell Kendrick, 84, both sold off their family farms long ago. But when the two get together for a family reunion at a relative's home in Scandia, the conversation turns to cows. "That's what happens when old farmers get together," Broecker says. "They talk farming."

Broecker: You were a little smarter than me. You quit in 1975, and I didn't get rid of the cows until 1996.

Kendrick: '96? You got rid of them that late? Well, I was ready to get rid of them. Well … I wasn't really at the time, but Bill St. Sauver come around. He just come in the barn one morning. I's milking and he says, 'I heard you want to sell your farm.' I says, 'That's news to me.' When I was through milking, I says, 'Come on in and we'll have breakfast and, you know, talk it over. Tell me what you have in mind.' That's the way it started.

Broecker: So he just walked in there?

Kendrick: Yeah, just walked in. I had no idea he was coming. I had no idea to sell them at that time. What made it pretty good is I didn't have to sell machinery or anything.

Broecker: Didn't have to have an auction then?

Kendrick: No. Just sold it lock, stock and barrel. Not a bad way to do it.

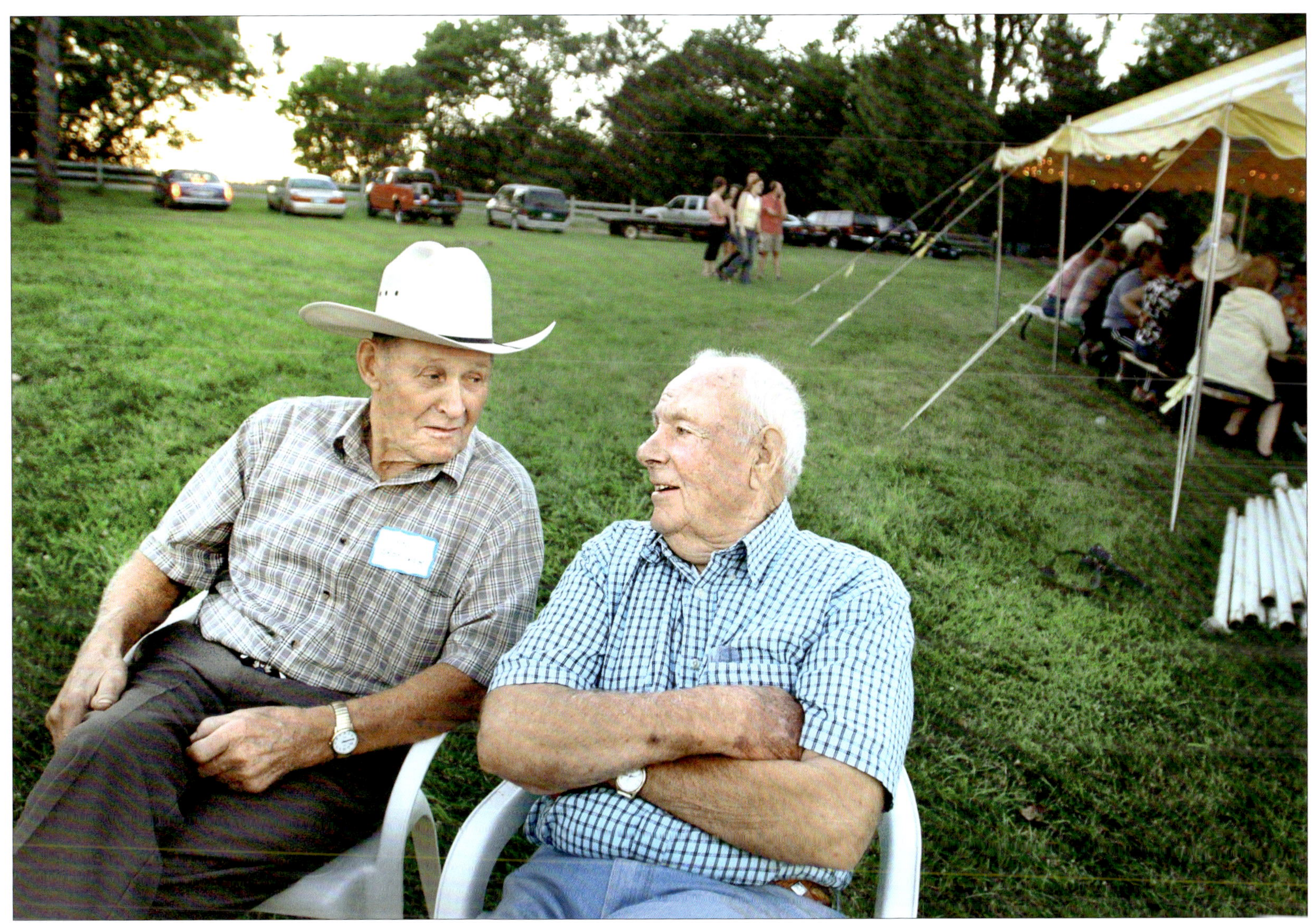

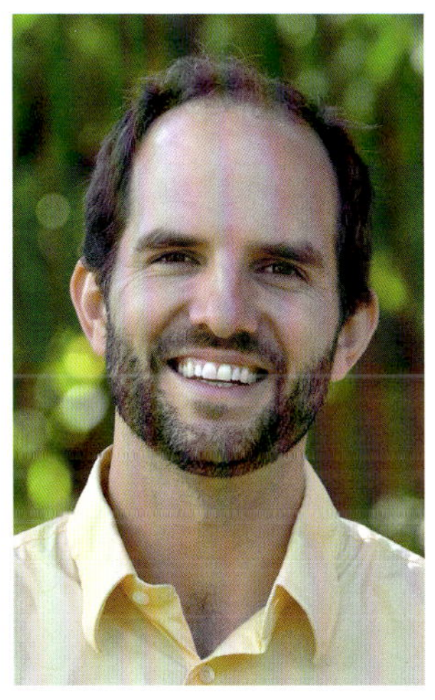

BEN GARVIN is a staff photographer for the *Pioneer Press* in St. Paul, Minnesota. His work has appeared in *Time*, *Newsweek*, the *New York Times*, the *Washington Post*, and other publications. He was named 2007 Minnesota Photographer of the Year and has received first place awards from the Associated Press, the National Press Photographers Association, and the Society for Newspaper Design for his still and video photography. Previously Garvin worked for the *Star Tribune* in Minneapolis, the *Christian Science Monitor* in Boston, and the *Concord Monitor* in New Hampshire, where he was named New Hampshire Photographer of the Year three times. Garvin grew up in Fayetteville, Arkansas, studied creative writing at the University of Arkansas, and earned a bachelor's degree in visual journalism from the Rochester Institute of Technology in Rochester, New York. He lives in South Minneapolis with his wife Jessica and sons Arthur and Lewis.